EUROPEAN PROJECT MANAGEMENT HANDBOOK

Techniques to write, manage and report projects supported by European direct funds

Edited by

Gianluca Coppola

ISBN-13: 978-153989199
ISBN-10: 1539891992

To my mother Annamaria, my father Benito, my brother Francesco, simply, thank you for all. To my wife Tunde, my sons Akos and Aron. You're the lifeblood of my life

Table of contents

INTRODUCTION

This manual has the primary objective of promoting skills in project cycle management, that career path followed by those who aspire to become a professional in the use of European direct funds, thanks to the redaction of proposals and, in case of approval, to the project management. The text was written and designed specifically for those who approach this world for the first time. I deliberately chose the less technical language possible, with the same rigor of information, and I often used examples and patterns to express the concepts and to suggest the methods to follow. I hope to be successful in enthusing the reader, rather than scaring him. European direct funds represent a complex world, certainly, but just as fascinating for the employment opportunities it offers and also for the challenges that everyday people working in this sector face. Those who work with European funds, soon learn that the new boundaries of reference are no longer those of their own country but those of the entire Union and beyond. Colleagues may be thousands of kilometers away and multiculturalism becomes part of everyday life of the European project designer.

Italy has always encountered historical difficulties asserting itself as a winner of direct funds through the presentation of successful projects. Statistics show that our country, although high on the number of projects won and then direct funds attracted, has to work more than the others to "bring home the bacon." In other words, we have to present more projects than the others to maintain the average. I explain all this as difficulties in European projects design: some countries despite presenting fewer projects have higher success rates. This means that they are better than us simply in "writing" the project. One thing I would like to be sure not to be misunderstood: Italy is not afraid to confront the other countries, with regard to the excellence of the ideas presented, to require European funding, but that is not enough, we must also know how to present these ideas to the European Commission and indirectly to evaluators who are called to judge. In other words, you must learn to write better European projects!

Good English, good basics of project writing and management, excellent negotiation and networking skills, are the three pillars on which to build a successful career in European project design. Anyone can work on these aspects to learn them and improve them. My contribution through the manual is mainly focused on the second pillar, the one containing the methodology, the technicalities. The content is made more "friendly" thanks to numerous practical tips and examples, in order to make more practical and less theoretical the transfer of concepts in such a way that, if you wish to try your hand at writing or participating in a European project, you do it by entering by the front door, that of excellence. When that happens, I'll be pleased to think that it was also because of this manual.

Gianluca Coppola

Author's Note

This manual consists of four sections:

1. In the first one are presented briefly the institutions of the European Union, the EU budget and the types of funds available;
2. In the second one is presented the methodological background in order to design, write and present European projects;
3. The third section provides a guide to the proper management and implementation of European projects;
4. The last section focuses on the administrative and financial reporting.

The appendix contains a summary of the Funding programs cited in the text with a brief description of them and references to official websites for further details.

SECTION 1
EU AND EUROPEAN FUNDING

1. Brief history of the European Union[1]

1945-1959: A peaceful Europe – the first steps towards cooperation

1949: after the second World War, France, the UK and the Benelux countries decided to set up the Council of Europe and called for the cooperation of Denmark, Ireland, Italy, Norway and Switzerland to prepare the statute of the Council. [2]
1950: Robert Schuman (French Foreign Minister) presented the Schuman Plan that proposed to integrate the coal and steel industries of Western Europe. Belgium, France, Luxembourg, Italy, Netherlands and Germany subscribed to the Schuman Declaration, whose objective was the creation of a European Coal and Steel Community (ECSC), thus putting into common national production of these materials. The CZECH was the first of a series of supranational European institutions, which would lead to what is called today "European Union".[3]
1951: The "Six" (Belgium, France, Germany, Italy, Luxembourg, Netherlands) signed the Treaty of Paris establishing the European Coal and Steel Community (ECSC). [4]
1957: The Treaties establishing the European Economic Community (EEC) and the European Atomic Energy Community (Euratom) were signed by the "Six" (Belgium, France, Germany, Italy, Luxembourg, Netherlands) in Rome, from which comes the name still in use, the "Treaty of Rome". The EEC had in its goals the economic union of its members (Belgium, France, Italy, Luxembourg, Netherlands and West Germany), to lead to an eventual political union.

---

[1] http://europa.eu/about-eu/eu-history/
[2] http://europa.eu/about-eu/eu-history/1945-1959/1949/index_en.htm
[3] http://europa.eu/about-eu/eu-history/1945-1959/1949/index_en.htm
[4] http://europa.eu/about-eu/eu-history/1945-1959/1957/index_en.htm

It worked for the free movement of goods, services, workers and capital, for the abolition of cartels and to develop joint policies in the field of labor and mutual social welfare, agriculture, transport and foreign trade.

1960-1969: The "fabulous 60s" - a period of economic growth

1962: The EU began to formulate the Common Agricultural Policy, which ensures that farmers receive equal payment for their products and that countries could exercise joint control over food production.
This created an enormous economic growth and a consequent overproduction of food.
1968: The six countries participating removed customs duties on imported goods.
The abolition of internal customs barriers was combined with a mark-up of the same duties for other countries, making Europe the world's largest trade group.

1970-1979: A growing community - the first enlargement

1972: Denmark, United Kingdom and Ireland entered the EU.
1974: the European Regional Development Fund (ERDF) was created to bridge the differences between the poorest and the richest regions.
The ERDF promotes economic and social cohesion by correcting the main regional imbalances and participating in the development and conversion of regions.
1979: EU citizens can for the first time directly elect the members of the European Parliament, which until then were delegated by national parliaments.
Since then, Parliament's influence began to increase exponentially.

1980-1989: The changing face of Europe - the fall of the Berlin Wall

Greece became the 10th member of the EU in 1981. Spain and Portugal followed five years later. In 1986 the Single European Act was signed. This treaty laid the basis for an extensive six-year program, designed to solve the problems of the free flow of trade within Europe and introduced the "Single Market". There was an enormous political shock on November 9, 1989, when the Berlin Wall was torn down and the border between East Germany and West Germany was eliminated, leading to the reunification of Germany in October 1990.

1990-1999: A Europe without frontiers

With the disappearance of the communist regime in central and eastern Europe, Europeans got even closer. In 1993 the Single Market was completed with "The Four Freedoms" regarding the movement of goods, services, people and capital. The 90s were also the decade of the treaties: the Maastricht Treaty in 1993 and the Treaty of Amsterdam in 1999. It began to give greater weight to issues such as environmental defence and protection, but also a greater emphasis on a joint action by European countries in the field of security and defense.
In 1995 three members joined, Austria, Finland and Sweden. A small town in Luxembourg attributed its name to the Schengen Agreement, which allowed people to travel without passport control at the border.

2000-2009: Further expansion

The euro became the new currency for 11 European Countries, which on 1 January 2015 became 19. 11 September 2001 became synonymous with "the war on terror" after three hijacked planes were flown into buildings in New York and Virginia. European countries began to work more closely together to fight crime. The political divisions between Eastern and Western Europe were reconciled, when more than 10 new countries joined the EU in 2004, followed by another two in 2007.

A financial crisis hit the global economy in September 2008, bringing ever closer cooperation among European countries. The Lisbon Treaty was ratified by all European countries before entering into force on 1 December 2009. It equipped Europe with modern institutions and more efficient working methods.

2010-Today: A decade of challenges and opportunities

The new decade begins not only with a severe economic crisis, but also with the hope that investment in new green technologies, designed in accordance with the climate and the environment, along with closer cooperation, will bring sustainable growth and prosperity. In 2010 the Union therefore launched a ten-year strategy for growth and jobs called Europe 2020.

This strategy is designed not only to overcome the crisis from which the economies of many countries are now gradually emerging, but also wants to fill in the gaps of our model of growth and create the conditions for more intelligent, sustainable and inclusive growth.

The EU has five quantitative targets to be achieved by the end of 2020 that affect employment, research and development, climate and energy, education, social integration and poverty reduction.

The strategy also includes seven priority initiatives that outline a framework within which the EU and national governments are supporting each other's efforts to achieve the Europe 2020 priorities, such as innovation, digital economy, employment, youth, industrial policy, poverty and the efficient use of resources.
Other levers of the EU, such as the single European market, the European budget and the foreign policies contribute to achieve the objectives of the Europe 2020 strategy.
For more information:
http://ec.europa.eu/europe2020/index_it.htm

2. The main EU institutions

The European Parliament

The European Parliament is the only EU body to be directly elected and represents one of the largest assemblies of the democratic world. The plenary sessions are held in Brussels and in Strasbourg, while committee meetings are always held in Brussels. Luxembourg is instead the headquarters of the General Secretariat of the European Parliament.
Its members (often abbreviated as MPE, Members of the European Parliament or in English MEPs) represent the citizens of the EU. They are elected every five years by the entitled persons belonging to EU Member States. In recent decades there has been consistent growth of the powers of the European Parliament and the entry into force of the Treaty of Lisbon has defined its role as co-legislator for almost all EU legislation.
Like all other national parliaments, the European Parliament is organized into committees (Agriculture, Economic Affairs, Environment, Foreign Affairs, etc.), There are national delegations for relations with all third countries and,

transversely to these two bodies, there are political groups, to which every national party reports and decides to belong.
The plenary session is chaired by the President of the European Parliament and the 14 Vice-Presidents, each of which deals with a specific issue that relates to the activities of Parliament and its functioning.
The President, elected according to the principle of alternation by the political groups for a two-and-a-half-year term, oversees the work of the Parliament and its constituent bodies (Bureau and Conference of Presidents of the political groups). Every year there are twelve partial plenary sessions in Strasbourg and six more sessions in Brussels (the two seats of Parliament, plus the administrative offices in Luxembourg).

The main powers of the European Parliament are:

Legislative powers: the Parliament shares these powers equally with the Ministers of the Council of the European Union for more than two thirds of European legislation, through the co-decision procedure, which concerns the discussion of a legislative proposal written by the European Commission. The Committee shall assess the legislative proposal and makes changes which are then voted in the plenary session. The Council then gives its consent to the proposal as amended by Parliament, or its disagreement, opening the possibility of a second reading.
The Parliament, in some cases, has the right to consent with respect to the decisions of the Council (position of assent or dissent) or consultative right (non-binding opinions).

Political powers: being the expression of European citizens and the only directly elected body, the political influence of the European Parliament is very high. With its reports,

recommendations and questions, addressed to the various actors of the EU, MEPs have significant influence, such as putting pressure on the Commission and the Council for action on human rights.
Parliament adopts reports also elaborated on "own initiative", which could be addressed to the Commission to bring forward legislation in a specific area or to provide in advance a concrete proposal regarding the different initative implementation methods.

Financial powers: the European Parliament is, together with the Council, responsible for decisions on the annual budget. The EU aims to set a long-term financial budget, indicating the highest levels of spending over a period of seven years (Framework Programmes). No agreement on these financial perspectives can be reached without the approval of Parliament that decides the maximum allocation to each budget item and identifies policy priorities. Parliament has the responsibility of monitoring the Union's expenditure on a permanent basis and decides whether to grant proxies (or clear the accounts) of all the EU institutions to implement the budget.
Website:
http://www.europarl.europa.eu/aboutparliament/en/00b3f21266/At-your-service.html.

The European Council

The European Council defines the general political direction and priorities of the European Union, representing the voice of national governments, but does not exercise any legislative function unlike the Council of the EU (see next paragraph). It includes the heads of state or government of the EU Member

States, together with the President of the European Commission and the President of the Council of the European Union. The High Representative for Foreign Affairs also takes part in the meetings.

Except in cases where the Treaties provide otherwise, decisions of the European Council are taken by consensus. In some cases, it adopts decisions by unanimity or by qualified majority, depending on what the Treaty provides.

The European Council elects its President by qualified majority. The presidential mandate lasts two-and-a-half-years, renewable only once.

The European Council usually meets in Brussels, in the Justus Lipsius building, assisted by a General Secretariat of the Council. Meetings, usually called EU summits are chaired by the President and take place at least twice a year.

Website: http://www.consilium.europa.eu/en/european-council/.

The Council of the European Union

The Council of the European Union is based on the intra-government principle, as it represents the interests of all Member States participating in their national ministerial level.

There are ten configurations within the Council: General Affairs and External Relations; Economic and Financial Affairs; Cooperation in the fields of justice and home affairs; Employment, Social Policy, Health and Consumer protection; Competitiveness; Transport; Telecommunications and Energy; Agriculture and Fisheries; Environment; Education, Youth and Culture.

Not to be confused with the European Council (see paragraph above), which has no legislative power but is a political and strategic authority.

Council meetings are organized by the Member States which maintain the presidency of the EU Council for a period of six months, with a rotation mechanism.

The order of succession in the Presidency is determined in advance and the country in charge sets the agenda and priorities of the Council, influencing the path taken by the whole Union. The headquarters of the Council are in Brussels for formal meetings, but some meetings take place in Luxembourg. The informal Council meetings are held traditionally in the country holding the presidency.

The EU Council has three essential functions:

The power to legislate: the Council shares this power with the European Parliament. In most situations European laws are developed through the co-decision procedure. This means that the Council and Parliament adopt proposals jointly, on the basis of a proposal from the European Commission.

Coordination of economic policies of the Member States: each year the Council draws up guidelines for the economic policies of the Member States, which then become recommendations; their implementation by Member States is supervised by the Council.

The power to approve the EU budget: this power is shared with the Parliament, which oversees EU spending and also adopts the annual budget for the EU. The Council has the final say on expenditure related to major European funding programs, which are the European Regional Development Fund, the European Social Fund, the programs on education and culture, programs for humanitarian aid and refugees, etc.

Website: http://www.consilium.europa.eu/en/council-eu/.

The Court of Auditors

The European Court of Auditors was established in 1977 with the task of auditing EU finances. The Court submits to audit the EU budget both in terms of revenue and expenses.

The composition of the Court is made of one representative per Member State: Members are appointed by the Council, after consulting Parliament, for renewable periods of six years, and choose one of them as President for a period of three years (also renewable).

Its main tasks are to:

- carry out an audit of the revenues and expenditures of the EU;
- check any person or organization handling EU funds, also making spot checks;
- describe findings and recommendations in the audit reports intended for the European Commission and national governments;
- report suspected cases of fraud, corruption or other illegal activity to the European Anti-Fraud Office (OLAF);
- produce an annual report to the European Parliament and the EU Council;
- give its opinion as an expert to the EU policy makers;

The Court of Auditors also publishes opinions on the preparatory work that will have an impact on EU financial management. To be effective, the Court must be independent from the institutions and bodies it controls. To this end, it is free to decide what to test, the manner in which to perform it, the form and the timing with which to present the results.

The audit work of the Court is primarily focused on the European Commission - the main institution responsible for implementing the EU budget. The Court also works closely with national authorities.

Website:http://europa.eu/about-eu/institutions-bodies/court-auditors/index en.htm.

The European Central Bank

The European Central Bank (ECB) manages the euro and defines and implements economic and monetary policies. Its main task is to **maintain price stability**, thereby promoting growth and employment.

The ECB is based in Frankfurt (Germany) and was set up on 1 June 1998 by the Treaty on European Union.

The main objectives are to:

- maintain price stability (keeping inflation under control), especially in the countries of the euro area;
- maintain a stable financial system, ensuring that financial markets and institutions are properly controlled;
- hold and manage the official foreign reserves of the Member States.

The ECB works in cooperation with the central banks of the 28 EU countries. Together they constitute the European System of Central Banks (ESCB).

Website: https://www.ecb.europa.eu/ecb/html/index.it.html.

2.1 The European Commission

The European Commission (EC) is based in Brussels, but it also has offices in Luxembourg, representations in all EU countries and delegations in many capitals of the world. The EC consists of 28 commissioners, each belonging to a Member State. The President of the Commission is appointed by common accord of the governments of the Member States, after consultation with the European Parliament. Once the President has been appointed, the government of each Member State appoints a

Commissioner. Then the Parliament must approve or reject each appointment.
Commissioners (and the President) are appointed for a renewable period of five years and each of them is assigned with a portfolio covering the area of responsibility (Culture, Transport, Environment, etc.): each Commissioner has therefore a connected Cabinet. The Commission's staff is organized in specialized departments called "Directorates-General" which are divided into directorates and units.
At the head of each department, there is a General Manager responsible to the relevant Commissioner.
There are also agencies that act on the responsibility and on behalf of the European Commission as executive bodies. They are located throughout Europe and provide specific services (for any reference to executive agencies, see next paragraph).
The Berlaymont Building is the headquarter of the Commission.
The Commission is often referred to as the EU "executive" or "technical" body. Core competencies are the following (although the list is not exhaustive):

Legislative proposal: the Commission initiates the legislative process. The European Commission has the sole right to propose new EU legislation (certainly based on political perspectives and observing social needs).
The legislative proposals of the EC are submitted to the European Parliament and the Council for approval.
Application of European legislation: the Commission's role is to ensure that European legislation is applied by all Member States (MSs): it can, in fact, initiate proceedings against MSs or private persons, whose conduct is not in conformity with EU legislation. The EC can launch a process that brings the

Member States in front of the Court of Justice in Luxembourg in case of breaches of EU legislation (infringement procedure).

Implementation of EU policies and the budget: the EC is responsible for the implementation and management of the EU budget and for funding programs approved by the Parliament and the Council.

In this perspective, the Commission will grant direct financial contributions in the form of grants to help develop an EU program or policy or to support projects / organizations which are of interest for the EU.

Loans and grants are awarded by the Directorate General of the Commission directly responsible for the relevant policy, from the offices of the Commission and the agencies that are scattered in Europe and / or other authorities acting on behalf of the Commission (Regional or National authorities, even in non-European countries, etc.).

International role: The Commission represents the EU in international negotiations that include the trade and cooperation agreements with countries outside Europe.

Website: http://ec.europa.eu/index_en.htm.

Fig. 1: The tasks of the European Commission[5]

[5] http://www.dadalos-europe.org/int/grundkurs4/eu-struktur_1.htm

The structure of the European Commission

In this document, the structure and operation of the EC are significant as **it is the Commission, with all its branches, which manages and disburses funds based on Calls for Proposals or Calls for Tenders** related to Funding Programmes. **It is important, then, to know the composition of the institution to which to refer for everything related to European project design.**

Because of the functions of the Commission in the different fields of EU policies and initiatives, its structure is complex and is divided into Directorates General, which act jointly providing general and specialized services. The Directorates General, as well as the agencies and the foundations established by the Commission are listed below. All information can be found at the following website:
(Http://ec.europa.eu/about/ds_en.htm).

1. Directorates General

Services

- Central Library
- European Anti-Fraud Office (OLAF)
- European Commission Data Protection Officer
- European Political Strategy Centre (EPSC)
- Historical archives
- Infrastructures and Logistics - Brussels (OIB)
- Infrastructures and Logistics - Luxembourg (OIL)
- Internal Audit Service (IAS)
- Legal Service (SJ)
- Office For Administration And Payment Of Individual Entitlements (PMO)
- Publications Office (OP)

Policies, external relations and internal services

- Agriculture and Rural Development (AGRI)
- Budget (BUDG)
- Climate Action (CLIMA)
- Communication (COMM)
- Communications Networks, Content and Technology (CNECT)
- Competition (COMP)
- Economic and Financial Affairs (ECFIN)
- Education and Culture (EAC)
- Employment, Social Affairs and Inclusion (EMPL)
- Energy (ENER)
- Environment (ENV)
- Eurostat (ESTAT)
- Financial Stability, Financial Services and Capital Markets Union (FISMA)
- Health and Food Safety (SANTE)
- Humanitarian Aid and Civil Protection (ECHO)
- Human Resources and Security (HR)
- Informatics (DIGIT) 22 23
- Internal Market, Industry, Entrepreneurship and SMEs (GROW)
- International Cooperation and Development (DEVCO)
- Interpretation (SCIC)
- Joint Research Centre (JRC)
- Justice and Consumers (JUST)
- Maritime Affairs and Fisheries (MARE)
- Migration and Home Affairs (HOME)
- Mobility and Transport (MOVE)
- Neighbourhood and Enlargement Negotiations (NEAR)
- Regional and Urban Policy (REGIO)
- Research and Innovation (RTD)

- Secretariat-General (SG)
- Service for Foreign Policy Instruments (FPI)
- Taxation and Customs Union (TAXUD)
- Trade (TRADE)
- Translation (DGT)

http://ec.europa.eu/about/ds_en.htm

2. **Decentralised Agencies**

Decentralised agencies carry out technical, scientific or managerial tasks that help the EU institutions make and implement policies. They also support cooperation between the EU and national governments by pooling technical and specialist expertise from both the EU institutions and national authorities. Decentralised agencies are set up for an indefinite period and are located across the EU.

You can find the list of bodies, as well as their contacts and referral links on the website of the European Commission: http://europa.eu/about-eu/agencies/index_en.htm.

3. **Executive Agencies**

The main mission of the Executive Agencies is to support the European Commission in the management of financial instruments that integrate European programs and are then established for a limited duration and must be located in the same place as the seat of the Commission (Brussels or Luxembourg)

For the European project designer it is very important to know the executive agencies, their functioning, the relevant Web site and how to get in contact with officials who work there. The reason is that these agencies are responsible for the development and publication of work programs and calls for proposals under the various funding programs. They are involved in the selection and evaluation of projects, they award the winners with powers of disbursement of funds and cuts where necessary. Executive agencies also organize numerous information and networking events, such as infodays and thematic conferences, conduct studies and produce publications relevant to the policy areas of the programs they manage.

The existing Executive Agencies are:

3.1 Education, Audiovisual, and Culture Executive Agency (EACEA)

http://eacea.ec.europa.eu/index_en.php

Its task is to implement a large number of actions and programs financed by the European Union in the field of education and training, active citizenship, youth, audiovisual and culture.

Despite having its own legal personality, the agency is headed by four Directorates General of the European Commission, DG Education and Culture (EAC), DG Communications Networks, Content and Technology (CONNECT), DG Migration and Home Affairs (HOME) and DG Humanitarian Aid and Civil Protection (ECHO), which remain responsible for programming, evaluating and issuing policies.

The agency is in charge of most management aspects of the programmes, including drawing up calls for proposals, selecting projects and signing project agreements, financial management, monitoring of projects (intermediate reports, final reports), communication with beneficiaries and on the spot controls.

The programs managed by the Agency are:

- Erasmus Plus: The new Erasmus Plus programme aims to support action in education, training, youth and sport for the period 2014-2020.

The actions of the Erasmus Plus program are divided into decentralized and centralized actions. Decentralized actions are managed in each country by National Agencies which are appointed by their National Authorities.

A list of National Agencies and their contacts is provided at the following link:

http://ec.europa.eu/education/tools/national_agencies_en.htm

Centralised actions are managed at European level by the EACEA. The Agency is also responsible for managing the Eurydice network, which provides data analysis and comparable information on education systems and policies in Europe.

http://eacea.ec.europa.eu/education/eurydice/index_en.php

http://eacea.ec.europa.eu/erasmus-plus_en

- Creative Europe: The new Creative Europe programme replaces MEDIA, MEDIA Mundus and Culture programmes.
  http://eacea.ec.europa.eu/creative-europe_en
- Europe for Citizens: the new Europe for Citizens program is a continuation of the previous program.
  http://eacea.ec.europa.eu/europe-for-citizens_en
- EU Aid Volunteers: this is an initiative that will bring volunteers and organizations from different countries to work together in joint projects.
  http://eacea.ec.europa.eu/eu-aid-volunteers_en

3.2 European Research Council Executive Agency (ERC)

The main aim of the European Research Council is to stimulate scientific excellence in Europe by supporting and encouraging the very best, truly creative scientists, scholars and engineers, who are invited to submit their individual proposals in any field of research.

The ERC consists of an independent Scientific Council and an Executive Agency acting on behalf of the European Commission.

The ERC Executive Agency manages the following tasks:

- to execute the annual work programme, as defined by the ERC Scientific Council and adopted by the Commission;
- to implement calls for proposals, in accordance with the work programme;
- to provide information and support to applicants;
- to organise peer review evaluation;
- to establish and manage grant agreements, in accordance with the EU's financial regulation;
- to provide assistance to the ERC Scientific Council.

http://europa.eu/about-eu/agencies/executive_agencies/erc/index_en.htm

3.3 Executive Agency for Small and Medium-sized enterprises (EASME)

http://ec.europa.eu/easme/

The Agency reports to 7 Directorates General in the Commission: Research & Innovation, Internal Market, Industry, Entrepreneurship and SMEs, Energy, Environment, Climate Action, Communication Networks, Content & Technologies, Maritime Affairs & Fisheries.

The European Commission has set-up EASME Agency to manage a number of EU programmes on its behalf:

- **Horizon 2020**: Research and Innovation; http://ec.europa.eu/programmes/horizon2020/
- **COSME:** Competitiveness of Enterprises and Small and Medium-sized Enterprises (SMEs); http://ec.europa.eu/growth/smes/cosme/index_en.htm
- **LIFE:** Environment and climate action; http://ec.europa.eu/environment/life/
- **EMFF:** Maritime and Fisheries Fund; http://ec.europa.eu/fisheries/cfp/emff/index_en.htm
- **Intelligent Energy – Europe** http://ec.europa.eu/energy/intelligent/

3.4 Consumers, Health, Agriculture and Food Executive Agency (CHAFEA)

The Consumers, Health, Agriculture and Food Executive Agency (CHAFEA) is a successor to the Executive Agency for Health and Consumers (EAHC), set up by the European Commission in 2006 to run

- the Public Health Programme;
- (from 2008) the Consumers Programme;
- (from 2008) the Better Training for Safer Food initiative.

http://europa.eu/about-eu/agencies/executive_agencies/chafea/index_en.htm

3.5 Research Executive Agency (REA)

The Brussels-based Research Executive Agency (REA) was set up in 2007. It began work in 2009, implementing parts of the 7th Framework Programme for Research & Innovation (FP7). In 2013 its remit expanded to include managing much of Horizon 2020, the EU's biggest ever R&I framework programme (2014 – 2020).

The REA reports to the following Commission Directorates-General:

- Research & Innovation
- Internal Market, Industry, Entrepreneurship and SMEs
- Education & Culture

and, as of 1 January 2014

- Agriculture & Rural Development
- Communications Networks, Content & Technology.

http://europa.eu/about-eu/agencies/executive_agencies/rea/index_en.htm

3.6 Innovation & Networks Executive Agency (INEA)

INEA manages infrastructure and research projects in the field of **transport, energy and telecommunications**.
http://europa.eu/about-eu/agencies/executive_agencies/inea/index_en.htm

3.7 Executive Agency for the implementation of the operations of the European Research Council (ERCEA)

The agency was created to manage only the Ideas program (part of FP7). However today it refers to the new Horizon 2020 program, always following the same goals. Like all the other Executive Agencies ERCEA is managed by a Director and a Steering Committee, both nominated by the Commission.

Its activities include:

- to execute the annual work programme, as defined by the ERC Scientific Council and adopted by the Commission;
- to implement calls for proposals, in accordance with the work programme;
- to provide information and support to applicants;

- to organise peer review evaluation;
- to establish and manage grant agreements, in accordance with the EU's financial regulation;
- to provide assistance to the ERC Scientific Council;
- communication.

3. The acts of the EU

For the European project designer it is very important to know the legislation and "soft law" issued by the various EU bodies, as the funds are granted under legislation and policies that the Union approves.

You must therefore be able to **justify the value of your project idea through a solid argument that refers to acts of the EU.**

Some funding programs are approved and implemented in the form of regulations, such as the EU Regulation 1293/2013, establishing the program for the environment and climate action (LIFE 2014-2020), or the Regulation 1291/2013 establishing the Framework Programme for Research and Innovation (Horizon 2020).

In other cases, the documentation refers to strategies and action plans, so one must be able to research and study the specific acts. For example, the Erasmus Plus contributes to, among others, the objectives of the strategic framework for European cooperation in education and training (ET2020): the reference document is made in this case by the Conclusions of the Council of 12 May 2009 on a strategic framework for European cooperation in education and training, namely "Education and Training 2020 - ET2020".

All the acts listed and described below are available in the Official Journal of the EU and are easily available online.

3.1 Normative acts

Regulations

A "Regulation" is a binding legislative act and must be applied in its entirety across Europe. To protect names of agricultural products, for example, coming from certain geographic areas or with specific names (e.g. IGP), such as Parma ham, the Council adopted a Regulation.

Directives

A "Directive" is a legislative act that sets out a goal that all EU Countries must achieve. The directive is binding with respect to the objective, but leaves Member States free to decide how. So, the directive must be transposed into national law and must be issued national standards for its application in each State.

This is the case, for example, of the Working Time Directive, which stipulates that too much overtime work is illegal. The Directive sets out minimum rest periods and a maximum number of working hours, but it is up to each country to devise its own laws on how to implement this.

Decisions

A "Decision" is binding only on those to whom it is addressed (e.g. An EU Country or an individual company) and is directly applicable.

A classic example is that of the Decision adopted by the Commission to fine the software giant Microsoft for abusing its dominant market position in breach of European competition law.

Recommendations

A "Recommendation" is a non-binding legislative act, which allows the institutions to make their views known and to suggest a course of action, but does not impose any legal obligation on those to whom it is addressed. For example, when the Commission adopted a recommendation which gave indications as to the employees of the financial sector, in relation to the fact that they should not encourage excessive risk-taking by customers, this did not have any legal consequences.

Opinions

The opinion is a tool that allows institutions to make a statement in a non-binding way, in other words without imposing any legal obligation. The Opinion is issued generally by the main EU institutions (Commission, Council, Parliament), the Committee of the Regions and the European Economic and Social Committee. While laws are being made, the committees give opinions from their specific regional or economic and social viewpoint. For example, the Committee of the Regions issued an opinion on how the regions should contribute to the EU's energy goals.
Website: http://europa.eu/eu-law/decision-making/legal-acts/

3.2 Soft law acts

The soft law acts are called atypical acts, in other words acts not explicitly mentioned in the treaties of the European Union; therefore they have no binding power on the legislative directly, but serve to address the legislative proposals, at

various levels, and express the opinion of the European institutions.
Each European Institution from time to time has adopted documents, which later became customary, in order to express their political opinion and action plans related to each topic.
In particular, the European Commission makes use especially of white papers, green papers and communications, in order to express its opinion about the action plans and the EU legislation.
Just by their very nature, soft law acts clarify the vision and the political orientation of the Commission, with respect to each topic covered by the various Directorates General; therefore they are a good tool to understand actions, guidelines and goals to be reached. Often they also clarify the direction taken by European legislation, explaining the objectives.
Soft law acts, then, can be a great tool for planning, especially in the preliminary feasibility analysis and consolidation of the project idea, in order to check if the orientation of their actions respond to the Commission's vision.
Taking advantage of soft law acts as a background for your own project idea, you can argue: the identified needs, the general and specific objectives to be pursued. Moreover, they serve to strengthen the consistency of the project idea, especially when it is clearly in line with European strategies, making the project current and relevant with respect to the EU in the various policy areas.

The most common atypical acts are listed below.

Green Paper

In the European Union and in general in the Western world, a "*green paper*" is an interim report of the government and a document for consultation and debate of policy proposals, which does not imply a clear commitment to act. A *green paper* can be seen, therefore, as a first step to change the law and can lead to the production of a "white paper".

Green papers are documents released by the European Commission to stimulate discussion on given topics at European level, inviting interested parties (bodies or individuals) to participate in a consultation process and debate on the basis of the suggested proposals. *Green papers* may give rise to legislative developments that are then outlined in the *white papers*.

Some examples of *green papers* are: the Green Paper on entrepreneurship in Europe (2003), on demographic change and a new solidarity between generations (2005). More recently there have been certain green papers on the European Strategy for Sustainable, Competitive and Secure Energy (2006). The complete list of *green papers* can be found on the EU official page which lists all publications from 1993 and earlier[6].

White Paper

A "white paper", is an authoritative report or guide, designed to help readers to understand the issues identified by the European Commission and how to resolve them. The *white papers* can be used not only in the political environment but also in business-to-business marketing.

The *white papers* published by the European Commission are documents containing proposals for European action in a specific field. In some cases, they follow a *green paper* published to launch a consultation process at European level.

---

[6] http://ec.europa.eu/green-papers/index_it.htm

When a White Paper is favourably received by the Council, it can lead to a European action program in the field concerned.
Examples of white papers are those concerning the completion of the internal market (1985), growth, competitiveness, employment (1993) and European Governance (2001). More recently, the white paper on services of general interest (2004) and one on a European Communication Policy (2006) have also moulded the development of European policies.
The list on the EU official website contains all White Papers published since 1993 and earlier[7].

Communications

Communications are the acts proper to the European Commission which have not, however, legislative authority or legal value, but serve to clarify the Commission's vision and explain its actions. Communications can trigger the actual legislation, inspiring it through the submission of action plans from the Commission, which decides to publish the report depending on the subject, directing it to the Parliament or the Council.
Communications can be both informative and adjudicatory, where the Commission has discretion, and also interpretative when the Commission announces rights and obligations expressed in the jurisprudence acts.
Communications can be sought through the portals of the various Directorates General, in the documents section, or through the general "news" service of the European Commission.[8]

---

[7] http://ec.europa.eu/white-papers/index_en.htm;https://en.wikipedia.org/wiki/White_paper

[8] http://europa.eu/legislation_summaries/institutional_affairs/decisionmaking_process/ai0037_en.htm

3.3 The Official Journal of the European Union

For full access to European Union Law you can consult the EUR-Lex website, that is the site of the Official Journal of the EU: http://eur-lex.europa.eu/.

The *Official Journal of the European Union* (EU-OJ) is the only periodical published every working day in all **23** official EU **languages**.

It consists of:

- **L (Legislation) Series** including **rules, directives, decisions and recommendations;**
- **C (Information and Notices) Series** containing information, preparatory legislative acts of the European Union, notices and adjustments;
- **S (Supplement) Series** is intended for publication of notices of **public procurements.**

As of 1 July 1998, it is repealing the printed form and is available only in electronic format on CD-ROM and on the Internet at http://eur-lex.europa.eu/.

The *Official Journal* series are published by the Official EU publisher, the Publications Office (http://publications.europa.eu).

4. European Union Budget and European Funds

4.1 EU Resources

The EU's sources of income include contributions from member countries, import duties on products from outside the EU and fines imposed when businesses fail to comply with EU rules.

The EU budget is made up for 99% of EU's own monetary resources, which are of three types:

- a small percentage of **gross national income** (usually around 0.7%) contributed by all EU countries - the largest source of budget revenue. The underlying principles are solidarity and ability to pay – though the amount may be adjusted to avoid over-burdening particular countries, the so-called compensation;
- a small percentage of each EU country's standardised **value-added tax** revenue, usually around 0.3%;
- a large share of **import duties** on non-EU products (the country that collects the duty retains a small percentage).

The EU also receives income tax for 1% from EU staff, contributions by non-EU countries to certain EU programmes and fines on companies that breach EU rules and regulations, such as competition law.

The EU countries agree on the size of the budget and how it is to be financed several years in advance, in particular through the **MFF or MFF - Multiannual Financial Framework**.

The MFF lays down the maximum annual amounts - ceilings - which the EU may spend in different political fields - headings - over a period of 7 years. It also sets an overall ceiling for total spending

The **MFF regulation (approved by the ordinary legislative procedure)** sets ceilings for **two types of** annual **expenditure**:

- **commitments** - legal obligations of expenditure which do not need to intervene in the same year but may extend over several years;
- **payments** - amounts to be paid in a given year.

In the annual budget process, the EU budget is decided within the spending limits of the MFF by the Council and the European Parliament on the basis of a proposal from the European Commission.

The purpose of the MFF regulation is to:

- ✓ translate political priorities into figures for the seven-year budget cycle (currently we are in the 8th programming period 2014-2020);
- ✓ ensure fiscal discipline for the EU;
- ✓ facilitate the adoption of the EU's annual budget through a multiannual framework.

4.2 Structure of the 2014-2020 EU Budget

For the period 2014-2020, the MFF sets a maximum amount of 959,9 billion euro for commitment appropriations and 908,40 billion euro for payment appropriations[9].

The MFF 2014-20 is divided into six categories of expense ("headings'") corresponding to different areas of EU activities:

Smart and Inclusive Growth

a) Competitiveness for growth and jobs: includes research and innovation; education and training; trans-European networks in energy, transport and telecommunications; social policy; development of enterprises etc.

b) Economic, social and territorial cohesion: covers regional policy which aims at helping the least developed EU countries and regions to catch up with the rest, strengthening all regions' competitiveness and developing inter-regional cooperation.

---

[9] Brussels, 2 December 2013 15259/1/13 REV 1 (OR. en) PRESSE 439 Council adopts the multiannual financial framework 2014-2020: http://www.consilium.europa.eu/uedocs/cms_Data/docs/pressdata/en/ecofin/139831.pdf

Sustainable Growth: includes the common agricultural policy, common fisheries policy, rural development and environmental measures.

Security and citizenship: includes justice and home affairs, border protection, immigration and asylum policy, public health, consumer protection, culture, youth, information and dialogue with citizens.

Global Europe: covers all external action ('foreign policy') by the EU such as development assistance or humanitarian aid, with the exception of the European Development Fund (EDF) which provides aid for development cooperation with African, Caribbean and Pacific countries, as well as overseas countries and territories. As it is not funded from the EU budget but from direct contributions from EU Member States, the EDF does not fall under the MFF.

Administration: covers the administrative expenditure of all the European institutions, pensions and European Schools.

Compensations: temporary payments designed to ensure that certain countries do not contribute more to the EU budget than they benefit from it.

The allocation of resources per sector can be found at this link: http://europa.eu/rapid/press-release_MEMO-13-1004_en.htm

4.3 The Negotiation Path of the 2014-2020 MFF

The negotiations on the MFF were held from 2011 to 2013 and involved three EU institutions: the European Parliament, the Council and the European Commission. They were held in two parallel paths, the political and the legal ones.

Regarding the first one, the 28 Member States have examined the key policies of "the MFF package". This path was divided into three phases:

- clarification phase in 2011: to allow a better understanding of the European Commission's proposals and develop the positions of Member States;

- negotiating phase in 2012: to reduce the gap between the Member States on key issues. In this phase has been identified a "negotiation scheme";
- final phase in 2012/2013: during which was reached a political agreement on the "QFP package" within the European Council in early 2013.

In parallel, the legislative process has seen the 28 Member States discussing in the appropriate preparatory bodies and Council configurations the technical elements of sectorial proposals. The work was carried out on the basis of the Commission's legislative proposals.
In November 2014, it came to completion, with the adoption of 75 legislative acts of the "QFP package".

4.3 Who manages and controls the EU budget?

The ultimate responsibility for the implementation of the budget lies with the **European Commission**, which is to recover all the funds unduly paid because of errors, irregularity or deliberate fraud.
National governments are also responsible for protecting the EU's financial interests. This implies their close cooperation with the Commission and the Anti-Fraud Office OLAF (French acronym for *Office Européen de Lutte Anti-Fraude*).
Also provided is a system of **checks and balances** to ensure that the funds are managed properly and in compliance with the rules, such as:
Monthly Reports: Every month the Commission publishes a report online, informing the Parliament and the Council on revenue received and expenditure incurred - so they can see how the annual budget is being implemented. This information must be available 10 working days before the end of each month.

Annual accounts: every year the Commission shall submit the annual accounts for the EU and for the Commission. They consist of: the budget (and its notes), the consolidated reports on the financial statements, the EU consolidated accounts which include the accounts of institutions and agencies.
The goal of these accounts is to provide a true and fair view of the financial situation for a given year. The annual accounts must also be clear, comprehensible and allow comparisons to be made between financial years.
The timetable for preparing and publishing the annual accounts is laid down in the Financial Regulation: provisional accounts are prepared and sent to the Court of Auditors for audit by 31 March. The final accounts are then approved by the Commission and sent to the Court of Auditors and the discharge authorities - the Parliament and Council – by 31 July.

There are also two types of additional controls.
Internal audits: Every Directorate-General (DG) has an internal audit unit that ensures the DG's procedures comply with the rules. They are free to audit processes, transactions, assets, etc. They report directly to the DG's Director General and also to the Commission's general Internal Audit Service.
External audits: Every year there is also an independent external audit of the EU's annual accounts and resource management by the European Court of Auditors. This audit takes the form of a report to the Parliament and the Council, which has the task of analysing whether individual activities and payments are conducted in a lawful manner and in accordance with criteria of fairness, but also the task of verifying the reliability of the annual accounts themselves, to assess whether they provide a "faithful" view of the financial situation. On the basis of this audit, the Court of Auditors issues an opinion – a 'statement of assurance' – on the figures

presented and the system and controls in place. The statement marks the beginning of the annual budget discharge procedure.

4.5 What are European Programs?

European programs can be divided into two types of funding: the funding managed directly by the European Commission and the funding whose management is delegated to the Member States indirectly through their central (national) and peripheral (regional or local) Governments.

Direct Management

In the case of EU funding under direct management, the funds are managed and disbursed by the European Commission based in Brussels or by an executive agency delegated, through calls published periodically in the Official Journal of the EU (OJEU).
The calls for the allocation of direct funds may follow two separate procedures: tenders (*Tender/Contract*) and grants (*Grant*).

Public contracts shall be awarded through a bidding process (*Call for tenders*) for:

- services: for consulting, research, training, transfer of know-how;
- supplies: for the supply of equipment or materials;
- works: for public works such as infrastructure investment, construction of civil engineering projects, etc.

The specific services, supplies and works requests are issued and awarded according to market parameters through "calls for expression of interest" with respect to specific programs.

Their publication does not follow predefined calendars. The Calls for Tender are accessible from the website: http://ted.europa.eu/TED/main/HomePage.do.
In the case of public contracts, the financing covers 100% of the costs, since the result is a service, a supply or a job for which the Commission has a direct interest, being the ultimate beneficiary.

Grants, or project funding, are usually assigned by way of co-financing through participation in specific announcements called "*Calls for Proposals*" on defined areas and about specific themes.
The main purpose is international cooperation in various fields: in fact, the proposals receiving grants typically require transnational actions, designed and implemented in collaboration between organizations from different European countries which join a project consortium.
Usually, subsidies or *Grants* cover only a percentage of the project cost, which can range from 50% to 85% on average (exceptions are found in Horizon 2020 and Erasmus Plus where the EC contribution can be up to 100%). The Commission, in fact, intends to support the launch and implementation of innovative projects for which it has a clear public interest, general and political, for their implementation. At the same time it requires the sharing with beneficiaries of the funding for the achievement of objectives, which can be substantiated in a project co-financing by the final beneficiaries. In this case the results and / or the end products will not be property of the EC, but of the recipient of the funding. The co-financing, in addition, is included in the more general responsibilities towards the achievement of the project results by beneficiaries.

In-depth analysis: the importance of networking

It is extremely rare that a single organization has at its disposal all the resources (human, technical, financial etc.) to execute a project in the most effective and efficient way. This is one of the main reasons why it is reasonable to adopt from the beginning a network view, creating synergies with local and European actors; thus any problems with stakeholders may also be eased by allowing wider distribution of risk. It is necessary to reason from the perspective of alliance, as this can address resource shortage, save time, improve the quality of project results and bring together expertise from different actors.

The reasons for adopting a network view are based on two main criteria:

1. dependence on resources
2. collaborative advantage

The first one is justified by the increased ability to gain power and access to key resources, the second is based on relational factors in which the exchange creates added value. Mutual trust, open communication, mix of skills and joint efforts are essential.

To build a partnership, you need to activate a strategic process that would not have the specifics of each project and that:

1. understands the needs implicit in the design;
2. defines the resources and the lack of capabilities;
3. identifies appropriate partners to then negotiate and conclude the agreement.

At this stage of planning should be considered the size of the partnership, that is, the number of participants, the length, the width of the planned activities, the

intensity, the distribution of responsibilities, the decision-making powers, the level of sharing of facilities and resources and the legal form.
Recognising the differences between partners is an essential step for a good collaborative process. It is important that all stakeholders are informed about why and how the cooperation is in the interests of the various partners. Making understandable the objectives shared by the partners is critical to:

- impart a sense of identity to the working group;
- clarify the relational mechanisms;
- define orders of magnitude and scope of activities;
- establish shared control procedures;
- prepare the ground for good communication.

You should also consider physical factors, such as proximity and distance, time zone differences, technologies used, size of the working group, social factors, that is the presence (physical or virtual), the different attitudes to team-working, implicit communication, mutual trust and above all cultural differences.

Indirect Management

Indirect financing is provided by the European Commission not to individual beneficiaries, but to national and regional institutions of the Member States, which are responsible for managing the assets and which act as intermediaries with the task of redistributing the funds received in their territory to beneficiaries each time selected.
The payment and management of the funds are then implemented by the Member States, regions, provinces,

institutions that also allocate additional resources under the co-financing form.
The use and control of loans are managed through the **National and Regional Operational Program** (**NOP** and **ROP**), public documents describing the priorities funded for each priority and each fund.
The projects are then submitted by applicants directly to the national competent managing authority.
The general aim of the Structural Funds and the Cohesion Fund is to coordinate the efforts of Member States to the development of their most depressed regions and provide them with financial support in order to promote a higher degree of competitiveness and employment.

The budget used for indirect European funding is allocated in the **Structural Funds** (**ERDF** and **ESF**) and the **Cohesion Fund**, which shall be executed within the framework of shared management between the Member States and the Commission. They can be integrated with other financial instruments such as funds of the European Investment Bank (**EIB**).

The Structural Funds and the Cohesion Fund are the financial instruments of the EU Regional Policy, also known as **Cohesion Policy**, whose purpose consists in comparing different levels of development between regions and between Member States. They therefore contribute fully to the objective of economic, social and territorial cohesion.
A single set of rules governs the five EU structural and investment funds (ESIF):

- European Regional Development Fund (ERDF)
- European Social Fund (ESF)
- Cohesion Fund (CF)

- European Agricultural Fund for Rural Development (EAFRD)
- European Maritime and Fisheries Fund (EMFF).

The EU countries manage the funds in a decentralized way through a shared management or by delegation from the EU to Member States. The websites of each fund provide information on funding available and the procedures to follow to request them.

This manual focuses on the access and the management of EU direct funds.

How to find information on funding opportunities

The Commission provides direct financial contributions in the form of grants to support projects or organizations that strengthen the EU's objectives and contribute to the implementation of a EU program or policy. Interested parties may participate in calls for funding, responding to public calls for proposals (*Calls*).

The grants and loans are awarded by:

- The Directorate General (DG) of the European Commission directly responsible for the policy;
- Executive Offices and Agencies of the Commission in Europe;
- Other authorities (national or regional agencies in different Member States or in non-EU countries).

The European Commission Website provides an overview, organized by sector, of all the funding opportunities available. You should also know and periodically visit the website of the specific program or National / European Agency managing it.

If you do not know the funding programs or offices responsible for its management, you may access the website of the

European Commission (ec.europa.eu) and click on "*Grants*" or "*Funding opportunities*". From there you can access a web page that contains links to all funding programs divided per sector, such as environment, culture, economy, energy, etc.: http://ec.europa.eu/contracts_grants/grants_it.htm.
Alternatively, if you know the program or managing body, you can visit the websites of the various DGs and Executive Agencies, searching the keywords "**Grants**" or "**Funding Opportunities**".
An additional source, from which to launch a search for open calls is offered by the Participant Portal of Horizon 2020. By clicking on the link "Funding Opportunities" it gives access to a huge database updated daily with information on a number of programs managed by the Portal.

In particular, here we can find information on the programs:

- Horizon 2020
- Research Fund for Coal & Steel
- COSME
- 3rd Health Programme
- Consumer Programme
- FP7 & CIP Programmes 2007-2013
- Other Funding Opportunities

For each program and related Call the portal offers us information on open, closed or forthcoming calls. A fundamental service in order to program the work time in the preparation of a proposal.
See for yourself the information extent by visiting the portal: http://ec.europa.eu/research/participants/portal/desktop/en/home.html.

SECTION 2
HOW TO SUBMIT A SUCCESSFUL PROJECT IDEA

---

5 Introduction to Project Cycle Management

Premise

The Project Cycle Management (PCM) was introduced by the European Commission in 1992 as a primary tool for the creation and management of a project, based on the approach of the Logical Framework. The first handbook, produced in 1993 and then updated in 2001 and in 2003, today is the result of several factors:

- The experience gained through the implementation of the new development policy;
- The issues raised by the current international debate on the effectiveness of the grants;
- The opinions of participants in the training on the PCM.

Managing a project through the techniques of project cycle management means implementing the action in stages, defining in each stage the role of the different stakeholders and the decision to be taken.

The PCM arises from the need to systematize the design which until then had not met expectations and had failed to achieve the objectives. Therefore to ensure the effectiveness of the actions, the European Commission introduced this approach which gives beneficiaries the key to the project, allowing those who develop the project to focus the proposal and its implementation on the real needs of the recipients, thus raising feasibility and sustainability levels.

The project cycle is based on three fundamental principles:

- Defines the key decisions for each phase, along with information and criteria for quality assessment;

- The phases of the project cycle are progressive, i.e. each step must be completed in order to allow the carrying out of the next one;
- The new programming and the identification of the project is based on the results of monitoring and evaluation, as part of a structured process of feedback and formal learning.

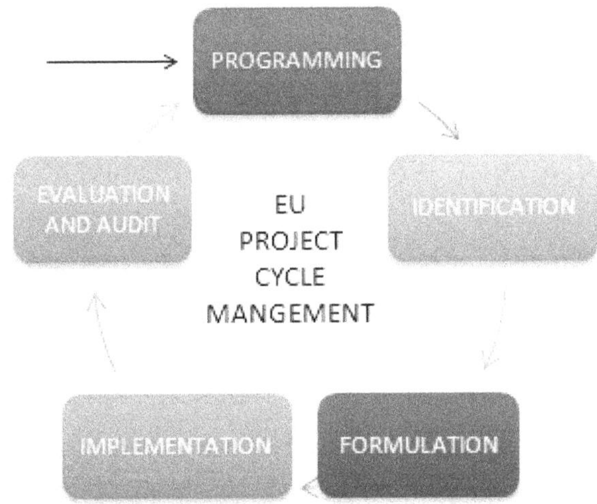

Figure 3: Project Cycle Management (author's picture) from "Project Cycle Management Guidelines" European Commission.

According to different definitions of "project", it is planned, interrelated and coordinated activities, in order to achieve specific objectives within a certain period of time and budget. The design action is developed jointly by a formal or informal group of organisations or institutions. Practically, every major project goes through a specific decision-making procedure called **Project Cycle Management**. The latter includes decisions such as key tasks, roles and responsibilities, key documents and others. The project phase/stage can result in either some sense of closure before the next phase begins, or it can result in certain deliverables which would provide the starting point for the next phase. The main phases of a project are usually grouped in *"work packages"*, and each of them includes a number of tasks organized and grouped depending on action type or time implementation. Thus, the transitions between work packages is the best time for evaluation and review of the costs and the project prospects.

Different organizations and institutions have adopted different terms to describe similar stages of the **Project Cycle**. For the EU projects in particular, one can distinguish between legal and managerial aspects of the project lifecycle.

- legal aspects refer to the establishment of relations between the beneficiary and the National Agency (NA) or the EU Commission. These address the procedures for project submission, contract conclusion, project monitoring, reporting, performance evaluation and audit.
- managerial aspects refer to the actual idea generation, project design, project implementation, including project planning, time- and team management, internal monitoring and evaluation, and reporting documentation among others.

These project lifecycle phases are shown in Fig.4 below.

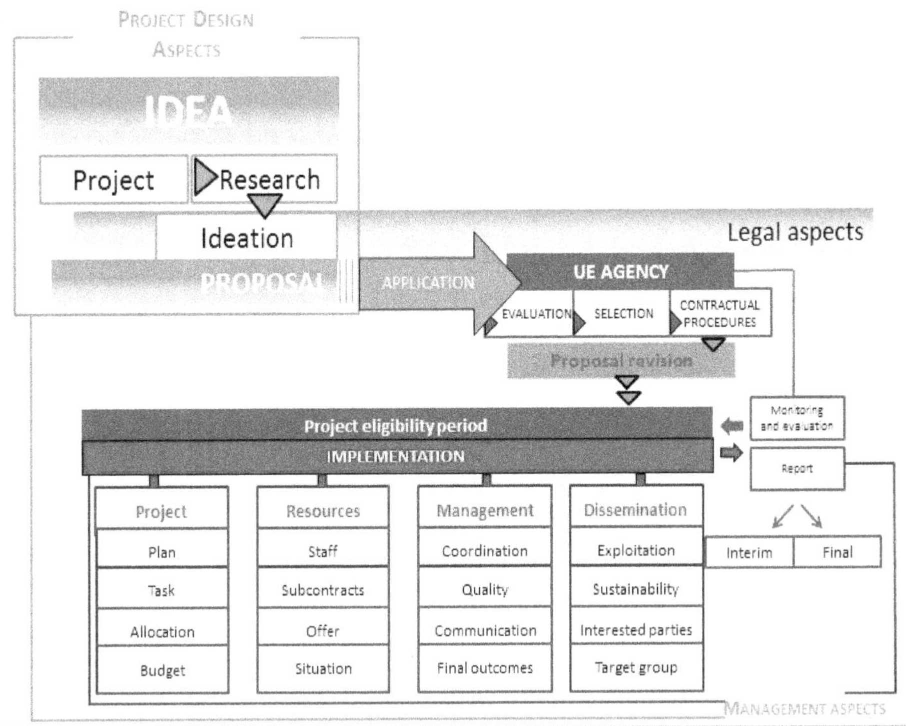

Fig.4 Project Cycle Management Scheme

5.1 Project Cycle Management – Design & Managerial Aspects

Here is one of the most commonly used categorisations of the managerial aspects:

1. Planning - there are three important aspects:

a) identifying the problem at local/national/European or sectorial level to form the project idea;

b) determination of the main goals and priorities to be achieved by implementing the project and

c) formulation of the methodology and the strategy.

It is essential that the project idea addresses a real sectorial and/or market need. Moreover, the planned results should be aimed at solving a particular issue of the selected target group. No project is successful, meaning sustainable, if its implementation is motivated by the sole desire to "get some EU funding".

2. Research – conducting background research prior to proposal submission is necessary to determine the project relevance, data availability and potential risks. It helps finding potential participants and relevant information to develop the project idea as well as to understand the sector's framework. Good background research reduces the risk of problems at project implementation stage, such as low data availability, incorrect assumptions and wrong choice of partners, among others. It also supports the generation/development of the idea and helps to design a relevant and coherent proposal.

3. Formulation – the appropriate ideas are then developed into a concrete project. It is essential to assess the suitability and the sustainability of the idea. The project proposal is to be designed and submitted in the official online and/or paper-based template, following the latest available guidelines of the NA/EU Commission DG. Furthermore, the project proposal includes detailed description of the project tasks and distribution among partners for each planned work package. Therefore, careful consideration and planning of all the activities and resources at a proposal stage is crucial.

4. Implementation – after the contracting authority has evaluated the project proposals, and the grant agreement has been signed. This is the longest phase of the project lifecycle, aimed at achieving the planned results as per project proposal. The implementation stage comprises: drafting of detailed management, evaluation, quality and dissemination plans, in order to ensure consistency of the project results. It also involves the following activities among others: preparing series of tenders (if applicable); signature of (including those for technical support); constant r and control over the spending, as well as the timely and quality implementation of the project tasks; financial and progress report drafts. Adequate project management is essential in terms of guiding the project partners and achieving quality results.

5. **Financial Management** – interim and final reports are required by the NA to determine suitable spending of the EU funding. In some cases, the Agency might require a progress report to evaluate the interim project implementation. The reporting should be provided in the respective template, usually available on the website of the reference programme.

5.2 Project Cycle Management – Legal Aspects

The legal aspects of the project lifecycle refer to the administrative support of the EU projects. In most cases each programme follows particular project cycle management logic; however these encompass more or less the following items:

1. **Submission of proposals** to the National Agencies or the European Commission DGs. These two bodies act as Contracting authority and Contractor respectively and each one of them has a specific operational field. The Commission deals with policy setting and programme design to be implemented by the NAs. EC and NAs have a mandate to control the whole lifecycle of the projects. The NAs are responsible for the implementation of all decentralised actions, whereas the EC DGs are entrusted with the centralized measures. Among others, the National Agencies have to support with comprehensive administration and to make payments to the beneficiaries.

2. Assessment of proposals – the project proposals need to adhere to a number of criteria (formal and quality elements, stipulated in the respective programme), which are used by the experts evaluating the proposals. Each proposal is rated based on a comprehensive grading system (see chap. 10 paragraph 3 and chap. 11 for more information).

3. Selection results – at this stage, all applicants are contacted. The successful ones receive individual notifications with the exact status of their projects, while the unsuccessful applicants are given feedback of the project gaps, weaknesses and potential strengths.

4. Contracting – successful applicants sign a Grant Agreement with the Contracting Authority, which stipulates the conditions for the grant award, the payment instalments, and the financial and operational responsibilities of each partner.

5. Eligibility period and project activities – during this stage the planned activities are carried on, the expenses can be incurred and covered only in the eligible period. This period depends on the duration of the project.

6. Project monitoring – the implementation of the project through its lifecycle is monitored by the Contracting Authority. The project progress is examined through regular on-the-spot project visits, convocation in the Contracting Authority offices, request of additional documents and Thematic Monitoring initiatives.

7. Reporting & Audit – beneficiaries are obliged to regularly submit reports to the Contracting Authority, which defines the accurate spending of the grants and the successful implementation of the envisaged activities. The required data should be summarized in specific report templates and financial reporting tables, provided by the NA or the EC:

- Submission of Interim Report – provides mid-term update on the project progress compared to the original plans and budgets; it is required only for projects of 18 months' duration or more; only upon acceptance by the EC can the next instalments be paid;

- Submission of Final Report - provides information on the entire implementation of the project, relating to the original plans and budget, the results obtained and the expenditures. The report assessment and rating are to determine whether partial or complete final payment would be made. The submission date falls two months after the end of the project.
- Audit - within 5 years of the final payment the National Agency or the European Commission may carry out an audit.

A very important aspect of the management cycle, especially for the new programming period 2014-2020, is how sustainable the results are after the project closure. This means that a European project should not only achieve its objectives, but it should also lead to sustainable and long-lasting public benefits – in other words it should ensure direct or indirect long-term positive effects for the EU citizens. Sustainability in this context means that crucial activities and results should be designed in a way which would guarantee that it would continue to deliver benefits to the target groups, structures, sectors or systems after the project closure. This underlines the necessity of a comprehensive review and critical analysis of both the project results and their relevance to the problem, stated in the proposal.

6. Introduction to the Logical Framework Approach for Project Design and Management

6.1 Overview of the Logical Framework Approach (LFA)

The US Agency of International Development developed in the late 1960's the *Logical Framework Approach* (LFA) in order to improve its project planning and evaluation system and to tackle planning, managerial, distribution of tasks and assessment issues. Among the challenges that were faced are: vague planning, unclear, immeasurable and unrealistic objectives, ambiguous management responsibilities, adversarial evaluation process and poorly defined project purposes. LFA turns out to be a successful solution to these issues, providing a core set of useful tools for high quality project implementation and assessment. Thus, the model is recognised by the EC as an essential part of the Project Cycle Management, officially used in EU project management since 1993.

6.2 What is the Logical Framework Approach?

The LFA is defined as an **analytical process** and a set of tools used to support project planning and management processes. The method combines a set of interconnected concepts and repetitive processes, used to support the structured and systematic analysis of the project idea and/or objectives. Basically, the LFA is ***'help for reflection'***, providing instruments for structuring and analysing a bulk of information to determine the key project questions, to identify the weaknesses, define the project rationale and pursued objectives in order to support the well-informed and sound decision-making process.

LFA however should be distinguished from the Logical Framework Matrix (LFM); the latter being defined as a ***tool***. In contrast, the LFA is an analytical ***process,*** incorporating analysis of stakeholders and challenges, setting of objectives and strategy selection. Indeed, while LFM or the so-called *Logframe* requires further analysis of the objectives, their implementation and the potential risks, it also provides a documented ***product*** of the analytical process. The LFM is made of a matrix with four columns and four (or more) rows, summing up key elements of a project plan, such as:

- Project Description or Intervention Logic: the project's hierarchy of objectives;
- Assumptions: the key external factors crucial for the project's success;
- Indicators and Sources of Verification: the way in which the project's achievements will be monitored and evaluated.

The *Logframe* also provides the basis for determining resource requirements (inputs) and costs (budget).

6.3 Link between Project Cycle and key PCM documents

How is the LFA used in practice?

- It is used in the identification phase of PCM in order to help analysing the existing situation, to investigate the relevance of the proposed project and to identify potential objectives and strategies;
- During the formulation stage, the LFA supports the preparation of an appropriate project plan with clear

objectives, measurable results, risk management strategy and defined levels of management responsibility;

- During project/programme implementation, the LFA provides a key management tool to support contracting, operational work planning and monitoring;
- During the evaluation and audit stage, the Logframe matrix provides a summary record of what was planned (objectives, indicators and key assumptions), and thus provides a basis for performance and impact assessment.

A common problem with the application of the Logframe Approach (particularly the preparation of the matrix) is that it is undertaken separately from the preparation of the other required project documents. This may then result in inconsistency between the contents of the Logframe matrix and the description of the project contained in the narrative of the main documents. The application of the LFA should come first, and then provide a base source of information for completing the required PCM documents. The LFA provides no magic solutions, but when understood and applied accordingly, it is a very effective analytical and managerial tool.

The scheme of the Logical Framework and other schemes described further, can be considered as methodological approaches, useful to those who are starting out in the world of design. After acquiring the necessary experience, concerning the compilation and use of these tools, however, they turn into a mental process which is almost automatic.

Strengths and Common Problems with the application of the LFA
*(**Source:** Project Cycle Management Guidelines p.59, European Commission, EuropeAid Cooperation Office, March 2014)*

ELEMENT	STRENGTHS	COMMON PROBLEMS/DIFFICULTIES
Problem analysis and objective setting	• Requires systematic analysis of problems, including cause and effect relationships • Provides logical link between means & ends • Places the project within a broader development context (overall objective and purpose) • Encourages examination of risks and management accountability for results	• Getting consensus on priority problems • Getting consensus on project objectives • Reducing objectives to a simplistic linear chain • Inappropriate level of detail (too much/too little)
Indicators and source of verification	• Requires analysis of how to measure the achievement of objectives, in terms of both quantity and quality • Helps improve clarity and specificity of objectives • Helps establish the monitoring and evaluation framework	• Finding measurable and practical indicators for higher level objectives and for projects with 'capacity building' and 'process' objectives • Establishing unrealistic targets too early in the planning process • Relying on 'project reports' as the main 'source of verification', and not detailing where the required information actually comes from, who should collect it and how frequently

ELEMENT	STRENGTHS	COMMON PROBLEMS/DIFFICULTIES
Format and application	• Links problem analysis to objective setting • Emphasises importance of stakeholder analysis to determine 'whose problems' and 'who benefits' • Visually accessible and relatively easy to understand	• Prepared mechanistically as a bureaucratic 'box-filling' requirement, not linked to problem analysis, objective setting or strategy selection • Used as a means of top-down control – too rigidly applied • Can alienate staff not familiar with the key concepts • Becomes a 'fetish' rather than a help

7. Analysis phase

The clarification of the system of assumptions, values and political framework to which we refer is the first step to be taken in the development of a design process. The conditions that will determine the actions and methodology of work should be clear. Defining the premises is necessary for the verification and is an act of transparency towards individuals who intend to engage in the network and the users of the project.

Different ways of interpreting reality and meanings that are attributed to it lead to knowledge, to different hypotheses, to operating modes sometimes conflicting; it is therefore of paramount importance to specify them and share them with those who will participate in the project. Defining and redefining the premises allows the development of the process of change. As in any field of human experience, you can not change what you do not know. Without this knowledge it is possible to take operational actions which can be incongruous or even harmful for the process of transformation, and without understanding "why".

The project ideas do not come from nowhere, but from history that day by day the organizations, individually and / or in groups, build in a growth perspective. Working consistently means to put our actions in a historical and experiential dimension, to tighten our work with strong links to the time, place and the communities where we are. Conversely you may have devised and written projects which are "beautiful" but "surreal".

The definition of the project idea often comes from being able to view and weave resources and human, relational and economic energies which have hitherto remained dormant and hidden with the desire for change. The important step is then to make explicit, with critical reading, the characteristics of the time and the community in which we act. In this sense all the work should take as privileged reference everyday life and must proceed in the sense of seeking the meanings that develop in it. Our projects are designed and implemented within "real context" of life.

At this point it becomes necessary to define what is the situation we want to change and how we would like to make it evolve, mature and / or modify. Operationally, we have to describe the problem and the situation, identifying the peculiarities, the source from which they are generated, how they manifest in the territory, what are the plans to change this.

At this stage we often speak about subjective perception of the problem because the data that you have on hand to make this reading are messy data, partial and not organized and are based on feelings.

On the basis of this premise, it should be specified that the preliminary phase to the writing of the project requires a process which includes the identification of potential stakeholders, in relation to the theme of the project, the identification of problems, the definition of objectives, the strategy to be fielding.

Strategies and tools for a successful implementation of the analysis phase.

Stakeholder analysis

As a first step, it should be clear that the stakeholders are the group of people, institutions, public and private actors who have or potentially can have a crucial role and interest in the success of the project. You must have a very clear idea who are the actors on the scene and how they could benefit by the success of the project, but at the same time understand how to meet the challenges that they could advance.

The tool that comes in handy is the SWOT analysis, able to define strengths, weaknesses, opportunities and threats (challenges) that are present in the context in which you are going to act. Finally, it is useful to have a clear framework for the subsequent allocation of duties and responsibilities between the project partners.

Strengths	**Weaknesses** ... ...
Opportunities	**Threats** ... ...

The problem analysis

The second step is to identify the main issues, useful to analyse the negative aspects of a given situation, establishing a relationship of cause and effect. This phase occurs in a very schematic form: the effect of a problem must be identified hierarchically higher, with respect to the cause, which should be represented below.

In this way, it will be possible to identify the real obstacle that must be overcome.

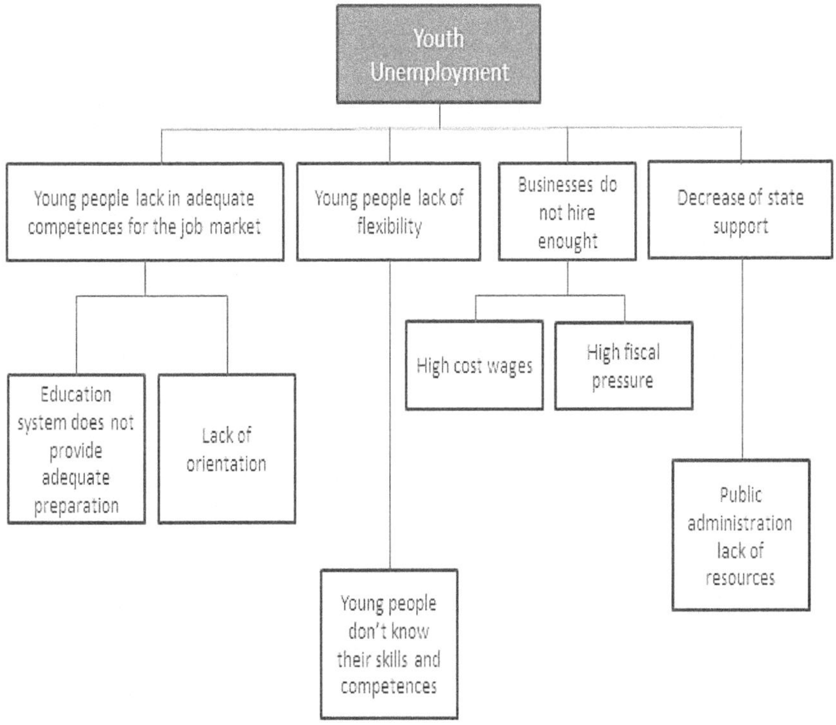

Fig. 5 Example of a Problem Tree (author's picture)

Useful tips:

- Try to conduct a comprehensive basic search in order to identify reliable information regarding the problem
- Potential resources via Web: official reports, publications, research papers
- If possible, conduct research via formal / informal interviews etc.
- Ask opinions of stakeholders and potential partners
- Be sure to consult several information sources to conduct a proper analysis.

Objective analysis

Starting from the definition of the problem, the first objective to be achieved begins to be outlined. At this point you should start to collect and systematize a series of information and data in both qualitative and quantitative terms that can be useful to give objectivity to our reading of the problem.

It is essential, during the identification and search of information, to define all necessary data for the construction of the project hypothesis and its future implementation, trying to figure out what data we need now, while writing the project, and what will be sought in the implementation phase.

A critical step is the analysis of the needs of the target groups of the project, which is a crucial element of the design. In fact, it is the moment when by reading "objective" data sought, they confirm or refute the perception that you have of the problem and / or the situation you want to change. Such cognitive activity provides insight into the phenomenon and allows good, consistent management of all the actions of the project.

To proceed to the identification of the objectives the problem tree should be re-consulted, analysing it with different eyes. All the problems that you can read should now be reformulated with solutions that go in the direction of positive goals. We can summarize this process in three basic steps:

- Reformulation of the negative situations present in the analysis of problems, in positive desirable and realistically achievable situations.
- Check of the relationship means-end, to ensure the validity and completeness of the hierarchy.
- If necessary, review each statement and bring goals at higher levels, erasing the objectives that do not seem necessary.

To better understand the links between the “Problem Tree” and "Objective Tree" that is, between two instruments of a single methodological approach to the analysis of the context, compare Fig. 6 proposed below with Fig. 5 above.

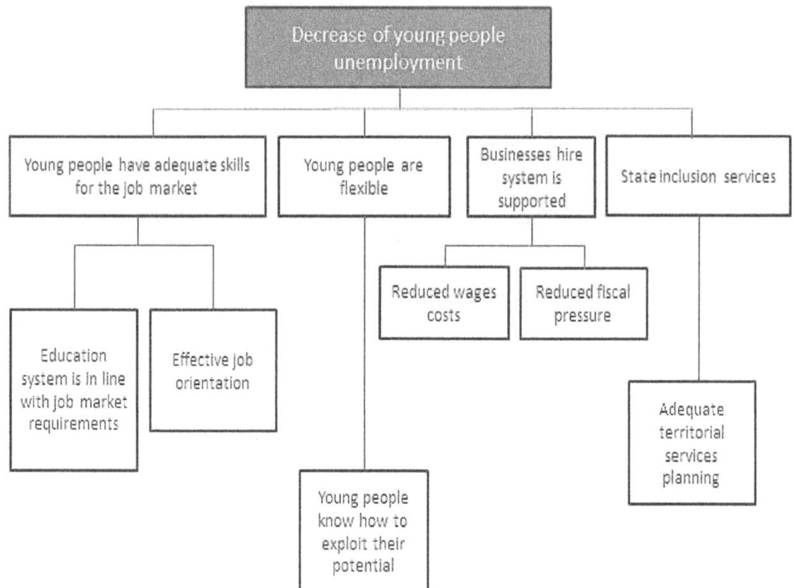

Fig.6 Example of an Objective Tree (author's picture)

Strategy analysis

At the end of the process of problems and objectives definition, we can have a clear view of the situation and formulate the strategy to be implemented, which will not be reflected only in the time of writing the project, but it will be an ongoing process during the lifetime of the project. The strategy should be seen as a learning process and you must be ready to reformulate it, if required.

Fundamental questions:

- Any problems or objectives should be addressed or only some of them?
- Which are the opportunities?
- What is the combination of interventions that supposedly will lead to the desired results,

promoting the sustainability of benefits?
- Is the coordinator of the project supported by local organizations?
- Which are the recurring costs and what can be realistically accessible?
- What are the most affordable options in terms of budget?
- Which strategy will have the most positive impact in terms of needs addressed?

It is also crucial to organize the data collected during the research in order to optimize the resources available and really needed during the design process. The table below can be a valuable tool for this purpose.

Useful data	Available	Not yet available data	Required for the design	To be sought during the design	Where to search	How

Finally it is important that the proposer formulates a statement of its *mission*. A *mission* is a statement outlining the reason for the project action, its identity, its aims and its uniqueness. This may seem unnecessary, as it is popularly believed that the designer is aware of the statutory purposes of the project. Often, however, the passing and the changing of time can cause loss of the sense of the original direction with the risk of developing projects that are inconsistent with the initial goals and therefore not linked to an overall strategy for the long term.

The statement of the *vision* and values, however, indicates the strategic goals to be achieved and the manner in which you intend to do so. This will make it clearer what is to be achieved in a medium - long term and how.

The purposes are to be understood as the long period purposes that the organization wants to realize, through the project. The definition of objectives allows then a first identification of the recipients, the type of intervention as well as the methodology. Each objective can be linked to one or more general objectives. Each general objective will be connected to one or more specific objectives. Please refer to the matrix of the logical framework for defining the general objectives / specific activities.
The logic is that of "Chinese boxes": the deeper you go in the specific, the more items will be defined more precisely.
The objectives will be:

- clear and understandable;
- measurable (especially the specific ones);
- achievable in a given time;
- verifiable.

Useful tips:

- Prepare an effective presentation of your organization and your team
- Approach the potential partner with a clear request on its role and level of involvement
- Express clearly the expected results, timing and support expected in order to allow the partners to make an informed decision
- Express clearly the responsibilities of the partners and establish appropriate expectations.

Check if your project idea works following these inspections.

First level of verification:

- The topic of the project idea meets the objectives of EU policies;
- The idea is innovative and / or complementary to any project: always check how many projects have already been realized in the same subject;
- The topic was covered in a sufficient number of investigations and is even "hot";
- You can clearly identify a target group, "beneficiaries", to which to address the results of the project;
- The topic meets the objectives and priorities of the call accurately without the risk of going "off topic".

Second level of verification:

- The idea lends itself to define a strong project strategy with a target, clear and effective objectives and resultswhich are able to be realised within the project timeframe;
- There are identifiable, even hypothetically, project partners which can contribute with their expertise to the implementation of the project;
- The project strategy implemented in the same goes in the direction of the objectives of the European policy / ies identified and you are able to prove it.

8. Task scheduling

8.1 The Logical framework

The results of the analysis phase are transformed and adapted in the planning phase into a concrete plan of activities and resources needed for their implementation. The stakeholders, problems, objectives and strategy analysis is used as a basis for preparing the ***Logical Framework Matrix - LFM***.

At this stage:

- You prepare the *Logframe* matrix, requiring further analysis and refinement of ideas
- You define the activities, the resources and the programming
- You prepare the budget

In short, **we move from the stage of feasibility and relevance analysis to the design stage itself**.

A useful tool to manage and supervise projects, the logical framework defines the functions of the project, the necessary resources and the management responsibilities. These elements are sorted in the first column of the matrix. In the second and third column, it provides the framework against which will be monitored and evaluated the ongoing progress (objectively verifiable indicators and sources of verification).

In practice, the Logical Framework (LF) consists of a table, or matrix, consisting of four columns and four rows. In the columns you can identify what the project intends to do, causal relationships are identified and you can specify the conditions and uncertainties beyond the control of the direct management of the project (Logic of Intervention, Objectively Verifiable Indicators, Sources of Verification, Conditions). The rows refer to the measurement of the effects of the project with defined key indicators and means of verification, and to the resources used (General Objectives, Specific Objectives, Results and Activities).

If used properly, the LF makes logical connections between activities, results, specific objectives and General Objectives more transparent. It should not be used as a fixed structure of mechanical procedures, but rather as a support to reasoning.
Practical example of Logical Framework that applies the assumptions described in the preceding Figures 4 and 5.

LOGIC OF INTERVENTION	INDICATORS	SOURCES OF VERIFICATION	CONDITIONS
Overall objective to improve the conditions of young people towards a full integration into the labor market			
Specific objective: to improve the education system towards the active recognition of their own skills by the young and a more effective approach to the labour market.	Full use of effective tools for orientation and recognition of skills.	Statistics, studies and direct surveys	Through the improvement of guidance and recognition of skills activities young people will be better prepared to self evaluate their skills and to position themselves effectively in the labour market
Expected results*: model of integration into the labour market and of support to the education system for training of tutors able to guide young people	% of young people entered the labour market who have followed the entry template devised	As above	Adoption of the model created by the education system and training of tutors
R1: Activities**:	*Means*	Costs	Conditions
1.1 Analysis of the education system in terms of instruments used for the orientation	Staff, equipment, training, studies, material, infrastructure	Source of Verification: Resolutions / Reports Meetings / Criteria for the identification	Implementation of the activities listed will allow the achievement of the main result of the

LOGIC OF INTERVENTION	INDICATORS	SOURCES OF VERIFICATION	CONDITIONS
1.2 Analysis of the tools used for the recognition of knowledge, skills and competences		of skills / training material / company agreements etc .. Costs: total EU budget xxxx - costs related to the first year	project and will be the foundation for the successful achievement of the overall objective.
1.3 Evaluation of the effectiveness of the tools by analysing the condition of young people NEET			
1.4 Analysis of the labour market and major changes			
1.5 Creation of an integrated school - employment model for the orientation of young people			

If you get the results and the conditions are met, then the general and specific objectives of the project will have been reached.

The *Logframe* is a useful tool for the design, but its use in itself does not guarantee the success of a project. Coordinators are usually required to summarize complex ideas and complicated relationships in simple sentences that are unclear or meaningless if processed in a superficial way.

Too often, in fact, the matrix of LF is used as a set of boxes just to fill, but beware: this attitude leads to inefficient design with unclear goals.

In addition, it is an iterative process, i.e. it does not end once and for all with the first draft of the *Logframe*, but you have to review activities and results when the implications linked to the necessary resources become clearer, that is, when writing the budget.

Useful tips

- Try to practice with the *Logframe* for various project ideas, so as to become familiar with the tool and make its use almost automatic.
- It's important to fill the *Logframe* starting from the top and then going down. A common mistake is to start activities, imagining them as the easiest thing to describe, and then defining the results and purpose. The rationale behind the LFA is the opposite: the general and specific objectives lead you to define the expected results, which in turn allow you to plan the necessary activities. The last step is to calculate the resources.
- Another common mistake is to confuse indicators and "targets", or goals and purposes. Remember that the indicators are intended to provide evidence that something has happened. So they must be clearly defined, measurable and realistic.
- When choosing or creating indicators never forget the "SMART" rule. To be effective the indicators need to be:
- **S**pecific to the objective that should be

measured;
- **M**easurable (qualitatively or quantitatively);
- **A**vailable (available at an acceptable cost);
- **R**elevant (relevant to the information needs of managers / evaluators);
- **T**ime bound (defined in time so you know when you can expect that the target is reached);
- Involve external people of different types and extraction, as partners, stakeholders, colleagues, to make sure that others follow the reasoning behind the matrix.

8.2 How to define, select and describe activities

Once the Logical Framework has been completed, you have to clearly define the activities of the project, so it is advisable to follow some simple but useful steps:

Step 1 - Make a list of macro-activities
The activities described in the *Logframe* summarize what the project aims to put in place to achieve its goals. These can be used as basis for making a list of the main activities, from which derive the secondary or complementary ones.

Step 2 - Divide each activity into operational tasks
The purpose of the division of activities into sub-activities or tasks is to make them sufficiently simple and easily manageable. The method is to split an activity into its sub-activities, take each sub-activity and divide it into tasks. Each task can then be assigned to an individual or a partner, even giving a deadline.

The main capacity at this stage must be to identify the appropriate level of detail. The mistake most frequently committed is to divide and sub-divide tasks with too much detail. The subdivision should end as soon as you get sufficient detail to estimate the time and resources required.

Step 3 - Clearly identify the Sequence and Interdependencies

Once you have completed the sub-division of the activities, they must be related to one another to define:

- The sequence: in which order the tasks must be performed?
- The interdependencies: does the activity under consideration depend upon the beginning or completion of another activity?

The question therefore is if they are preparatory activities to others and to provide a timeline and a logic to allow the smooth running of activities.

Step 4 - Make an estimate of the Beginning, the Duration and the End of Activities

Specifying the timing means making a realistic estimate of the duration of each task and placing it over time by defining a start and an end date.

Often you can not fix these dates with absolute certainty, but it is very important to have a clear picture of the interconnections between the various activities and the duration of each task, so you can easily re-program the start and end dates.

Step 5 - Define goals

The goals (***Milestones***) provide a basis for monitoring and managing the project. They are key events that provide a measure of ongoing progress and an objective to which the project team can aim, such as the completion of the main product or the closing of a key stage. The milestones are also used to have intermediate objectives and to establish moments of ongoing evaluation that correspond with the achievement of these goals.

Step 6 - Define the Skills

Once you have identified the tasks you can specify the kinds of expertise needed to achieve them. This step is very important, for example for the choice and involvement of the partners, which must cover all the skills and expertise necessary for the implementation of the project.

Step 7 - Assign Tasks to members of the consortium and working team

This step occurs at two levels: at consortium level it is necessary to divide the tasks among the project partners, or between organizations, while internally to organizations involved, it implies the division of roles and responsibilities between the people who represent the team.

This is a step that involves much more than simply telling everyone what to do. With the division of tasks the responsibility for achieving the goals is defined.

8.3 Practical tools for the planning of activities

When drawing up a scheme of the activities it is useful to have a graphical representation of the different actions of the project and the timing in which they will be implemented. This helps to identify their logical sequence, expected duration and dependencies between activities and provides a basis for the allocation of management responsibilities. Once the scheme has been drawn up, you can proceed to define the resources and program costs.

A useful tool to plan the activities may be the Gantt chart, a type of bar chart, developed by Henry Gantt in 1910, illustrating the project schedule. It is frequently used in project management and is one of the most popular and useful methods to show the activities in the temporal duration of the project.

The Gantt chart is built starting from a horizontal axis - a representation of the total project time period, divided into incremental stages (for example, days, weeks, months) - and a vertical axis - a representation of the tasks or activities that constitute the project.

Horizontal bars of variable length represent sequences, duration and time span of each individual project activity. These bars can overlap during the same period of time to indicate the possibility of carrying out in parallel some of the activities.

The scheme allows you to see at a single glance:

- What are the various activities
- When each activity begins and ends
- The duration of each activity
- If and when activities overlap with others and how long
- The start and end date of the entire project

In summary, in a Gantt chart you can read easily and quickly what needs to be done and when.

Task division	Year 1			Year 2		
	G	F	Mx	G	F	Mx
	1	2	3	1	2	3
WP1 - Project Management						
Task 1.1 Creating a simple management process and a project manual						
Task 1.2 Creation of project management system including the online one						
Task 1.3 Management and daily coordination						
WP2 –Development of the analysis methodology						
Task 2.1 Analysis of materials and content						
Task 2.2 Analysis of the tools for field work						
Task 2.3 Creation of the methodology						
WP3 –Needs analysis						
Task 3.1 Fieldwork						
Task 3.2 Production of regional reports						
Task 3.3 Needs analysis report						
WP4 –Development of educational contents						
Task 4.1 Identification and first classification of the material content						

Task division	Year 1			Year 2		
	G	F	Mx	G	F	Mx
	1	2	3	1	2	3
Task 4.3 Final selection of the content for training.						
Task 4.4 Treatment and adaptation of new materials and content for e-learning System						
Task 4.5 Identification and classification of materials and content concerning the Export Manager						
WP5 – Development of support content						
Task 5.1 Identification and first classification of the support content						
Task 5.2 Map of the support materials						
Task 5.3 Final selection of the support content for training						
Task 5.4 Adaptation of support content						
Task 5.5 Development of an online electronic glossary.						
WP6 -Translation						
Task 6.1 Glossary translation						
WP7 - Development and maintenance of the e-learning platform						
Task 7.1 Description of the technical requirements for the e-learning System.						
Task 7.2 Programming of the e-learning System						
Task 7.3 Integration of information, knowledge and training materials in the System.						
WP8 -Assessment and validation						
Task 8.1 Creation and validation of the assessment methodology						

Task 8.2 Identification and selection of participants for implementation and validation.						
Task 8.3 Organization of the training						
Task 8.4 Evaluation report						
Task 8.5 Implementation of the improvements mentioned in the report						
WP9 - Pilot test						
Task 9.1 Pilot Test						
Task 9.2 Evaluation of the pilot test in each Country						
Task 9.3 Evaluation of the pilot test phase						
WP10 - Dissemination and Exploitation						
Task 10.1 Development of the methodology for the awareness workshops						
Task 10.2 Organization of awareness workshops						
Task 10.3 Definition of the dissemination plan						
Task 10.4 Processing of dissemination tools						
Task 10.5 Implementation of dissemination activities						
Task 10.6 Final Conference						
WP11 – Sustainability						
Task 11.1 Processing of the sustainability plan						

In addition to the calendar of activities, in complex and transnational projects implemented by consortia of partners, it is also useful to have a scheme of task division that allows you to make a summary of activities, highlighting the assignments to partners and the different responsibilities. This scheme is often called "*Task division scheme*"

TASKS DIVISION	**P1**	**P2**	**P3**	**Px**
WP1 - Project Management				
Task 1.1 Creating a simple management process and a project manual				
Task 1.2 Creazione del sistema di gestione di progetto incluso quello online Creation of a project management system including the online one				
Task 1.3 Daily management and coordination				
WP2 – Development of the analysis methodology				
Task 2.1 Analysis of materials and content				
Task 2.2 Analysis of the tools for field work	x			
Task 2.3 Methodology creation	x			
WP3 – Needs analysis				
Task 3.1 Fieldwork		x		
Task 3.2 Production of regional reports		x		
Task 3.3 Needs analysis report				
WP4 – Development of training contents				
Task 4.1 Identification and first classification of the material content				
Task 4.2 Final selection of content and materials to be developed				
Task 4.3 Final selection of content for training.				
Task 4.4 Treatment and adaptation of new materials and content for e-learning system	x			
Task 4.5 Identification and classification of materials and content concerning the Export Manager				
WP5 – Development of support content				
Task 5.1 Identification and first classification of support content				
Task 5.2 Map of support material				

TASKS DIVISION	P1	P2	P3	Px
Task 5.3 Final selection of the support content for training				
Task 5.4 Adaptation of support content				
Task 5.5 Development of an online electronic glossary.				
WP6: Translations				
Task 6.1 Translation of the glossary and the dissemination material				
WP7 -Development and maintenance of the e-learning platform				
Task 7.1 Description of the technical requirements for the e-learning System.				
Task 7.2 Programming of the e-learning System				
Task 7.3 Integration of information, knowledge and training materials in the System.				
WP8 - Assessment and validation				
Task 8.1 Creation and validation of the assessment methodology				
Task 8.2 Identification and selection of participants for implementation and validation.				
Task 8.3 Organization of the training				
Task 8.4 Evaluation report				
WP9: PILOT TEST				
T9.1: Pilot test				
Task 9.2 Evaluation of the pilot test in each Country				
Task 9.3 Evaluation of the pilot test phase				
WP10 - Dissemination and Exploitation				
Task 10.1 Development of the methodology for the awareness workshops				
Task 10.2 Organization of awareness workshops				
Task 10.3 Definition of the dissemination plan				
Task 10.4 Processing of dissemination tools				
Task 10.5 Implementation of dissemination activities				
Task 10.6 Final Conference				
WP11 – Sustainability				
Task 11.1 Processing of the sustainability plan				

9. Cost appraisal: the budget

Appraising the costs of a project is the basis of its success and requires care and diligence as for the planning of the project idea. **The actions and costs provided in the project are closely interconnected: the actions reach their rationality through costs, while the latter find their raison d'être in the first.**

A correct and realistic estimate of costs also supports the design phase because it helps to understand whether the planned activities are actually achievable, effective and efficient.

The first step is to clarify the available resources, both from the point of view of the total funding that may be required and from the point of view of individual budget headings. Understanding the types of costs that may be incurred is critical to know how much we can push off with the project.

Then, it is necessary to estimate the resources required. We can divide the costs in general in two types:

- Variable costs: these vary in proportion to the volume of activities
- Fixed costs: do not vary depending on the activity

Each activity will be assigned a cost in relation to its nature. In order to plan the budget at best, a model must be provided that will help to identify the various items, the budget that we have allocated to it and to systematize the overall organization of the requested funding.

In order to provide all the necessary resources within the budget, you can follow the list of activities, assigning each the sum relating to its implementation.

The sum I speak about here is basically given by the assessment of costs in terms of human resources (who?) who will carry out these activities. Do these activities need a technical or administrative profile? Do you need the supervision of an internal manager or coordinator in the project or maybe in individual tasks? What daily cost does each of them have and for how many days you expect his involvement? Here, these questions and the logical process below will allow you to get an idea of the cost to budget for those activities.

In addition to the implementation activities associated with the staff budget, should be carefully budgeted management and dissemination activities, subcontracting, travel, any equipment, etc.

The project budget should allow the allocation of costs between the different funding sources so that each part is clearly related to its respective contribution. To make sure that the costs are as accurate as possible, you can ask for quotes or base your costs paid in the past for the same thing, if you do not have a clear indication of the amount that can be attributed to the single budget heading.

It is also essential to explain, during the project proposal, what were the criteria you used for the allocation of costs, including particular choices and / or conditions necessary to the award of a cost compared to another.

Projects co-financed by the European Union are subject to procedures of financial reports, the so-called "reporting". This involves the collection, organization and presentation of evidence of all or part of the costs incurred. The financial report must be accompanied by a report on the management and the realization of tasks and the description of the results.

Useful tips

Pay attention to costs (eligible or non-eligible)

- Always give a rationale, quantitative and qualitative explanation of the costs - even if not expressly required;
- Justifying where there are abnormal situations concerning the budget;
- If you are buying instruments you should describe the amortization;
- Assign subcontracts only to specific activities within the project - describe them with a sufficient degree of detail;
- A cost, to be reportable, must have been included in the budget, therefore pay attention to the "shopping list".

The drafting of the budget and therefore its management if and when the proposal is approved, depends mainly on whether the budget meets the financial rules to "real costs" or to "lump-sum".

All the features and the technical details of the two modes can be read in Section 4.

9.1 Types of funding

EU support may take the form of:

a) a pure lump sum,
b) a lump sum calculated on unit costs
c) a refund of a percentage of eligible costs.

Depending on the type of grant, it is possible to have a combination of all or part of these types of funding. A project budget shall be prepared in accordance with that amount.

a) In the case of grants awarded as a pure lump-sum, the beneficiary must prove that the activity for which it receives the support was actually realized and achieved the expected results, rather than the actual amount of the expenses. If the activity funded was carried out in a satisfactory manner, you receive full payment. In the event that the action was not carried out satisfactorily, (partial or total) repayment of the grant awarded will typically be required on the basis of the criteria established for each action. A consequence of this type of grant is that the recipient will receive a total amount not divided into sub-items of expenditure (e.g. staff, travel and so on.).
b) In the case of grants in lump-sum based on prices of unit costs (for example, daily rates for the stay), the beneficiary receives a lump-sum calculated but using values / benchmarks, indeed the unit costs that do not depend on subjective issues of the beneficiary. E.g.. I get € 500 per person per trip for distances up to 1500 km. If I travel two days or five I will anyway receive € 500 which is the unit cost that I have to use. Of course, programs that apply such rules also provide comprehensive reference tables from which you can easily calculate the budget for the action. Also for these types of grants the Contracting Authority assessment of the final report is mainly focused on monitoring the achievement of results and less to see how the budget allocated was spent to achieve those results. The fact remains, however, that the recipient must always keep in accounting and administrative project folders every track of how the money was spent, traces to be shown in the case of checks or audits.

c) In the case of the grant (or part of a grant) assigned on the basis of real costs, the beneficiary must keep and on request submit the proofs of expenditure (supporting documents) related to the expense items based on real costs. In fact, it is on that total amount that it will receive the reimbursement of a certain % of the amount spent. The EU funding will be calculated by applying a percentage of the eligible costs actually incurred. During the evaluation of the final report, if an activity is not completed or only partly, or the funding has been used for ineligible expenses, the grant will be reduced proportionately. Where the reported costs are less than anticipated, the grant will be reduced according to the percentages established in the loan agreement. Further details will be included in the documentation provided for the management of the loan agreements.

The European Union can finally offer financial support to cover part of the costs of operating costs of the main non-governmental bodies that promote priority issues in line with certain EU policies. The grant provides financial support to the operation of an institution (for an accounting period) in order to get it to perform a series of tasks that are fundamental for the local implementation of one or more programs or policies.

9.2 Types of eligible costs

The types of eligible costs are generally fixed and identical, whatever the program reference, although exceptions are possible. Always check the work program of reference. They fall into the following categories:

1. *Staff*;
2. *Travel and Subsistence*;
3. *Equipment*;
4. *Subcontract*;
5. Other;
6. *Indirect costs/Overhead*;

Concerning those categories, what can change are the management and accounting modes of relating budget and this depends if your project has a management on “real costs” or "lump-sum" with or without explanation of unit costs. (See steps from a) to b) of the preceding paragraph).
The various cost categories and the different methods of management and reporting will be widely discussed in the chapter dedicated to reporting in section no. 4 to which you should refer for further details.

10. Documentation Guidance

The system of call for proposals certainly has many merits and advantages. But the introduction of this method and the development of the forms have at the same time promoted a logic that could be called “project laziness”. **Basically there has be a change from a process of “idea - call identification - project - filling in the form” to one of “reading of a call - design of a proposal - filling in a form”.**
A project that was only put together because at that time there was a certain call and then behind that there are no detailed and reasoned ideas, would not make sense of the complexity of the process and the elements that compose it. Indeed, very often this approach, very common in actual operations, is in itself a harbinger of proposals voted for rejection because

based on a "forced" adaptation of the idea to the call available at that time.
The proper methodological approach, longer and requiring more effort and interaction skills, but also by far the potentially winning, is instead based on the process **"idea - call identification - project - completion of the form"**.
We will be working on the sequence in which to look for information, knowing that in many cases information is crucial for the next steps; indeed, in many cases, as we shall see, an information may determine the interruption of the call participation itself.

10.1 The "jungle" of documents and information

One of the most frequent obstacles encountered when approaching the EU funding programs is to be able to navigate the jungle of documents available on the web pages of the various offices of the European Commission, such as guides, work programs, attachments, forms, models, explanatory presentations and many other unofficial informative documents. In some cases, you can get to several hundred pages, but also in simpler cases we have to deal with dozens and dozens of sheets to fill out.
The first tip to follow is to download and view only the official documentation available on the websites of various DGs or Executive Agencies of the European Commission. Sites of information and guidance can be very useful to get a general idea of the calls and the strategic objectives of the various programs, but if you want to begin implementing the program it is always better to refer only to the official documentation provided by the funding bodies, to be sure to have access to correct, complete and up-to-date information.

Once you have access to the web pages of reference of individual programs or calls of interest, it is very important to select relevant documentation between the various materials available, in particular the following documents:

- The ***Call for proposals***: the notice is published in the Official Journal of the EU, or essentially on the sites of the DG or the National Agency and contains basic information such as a brief description of the purpose of the call, the eligibility rules, the deadlines.
- The ***Programme Guide*** and the ***Work Programme***: these documents are critical because they contain all the details that allow us to understand if the notice or the program fits for us. In particular there are: objectives, actions funded, any priorities, available budget, deadlines, eligibility rules, procedures for the submission of proposals, evaluation criteria, references and useful contacts.

The second problem we encounter is the way in which the contents are expressed (often with legislative and technical language specific to the topic) and processed graphically in documents or within the sites. In fact, who writes a call follows its own logic diagram with respect to the sequence of topics and themes and this logic not only differs from call to call but it is often different from that of those who read them. The problem is thus of orientation on one hand and of logical order on the other. That is, you must adopt a mental compass to navigate the "thick woods" created by the words, and at the same time, you must learn to choose the logical sequence through which to search and reorganize information. Finally, you must also pay attention to the translations of the calls in the various European languages: the national language versions are useful for quick access to information, but the English version is the official one, so in the case of small discrepancies, you must follow the original.

The first information to look for is the call deadline. It seems trivial and obvious, but it is not so; often you will be informed of calls, almost closed or even after the deadline. It happens, sometimes, that you read the call and find out only at the end (usually the deadline is never at the beginning of the text) that actually was a wasted effort.

There are several elements that you can find on the deadline. Obviously if the call has expired, you must figure out how long you have to fulfil all the actions related to that call.

But it's not enough, because you can also try to understand (in that call or in relating texts) if there are other possible deadlines; there are in fact some "open" calls, i.e. calls that have more than a specified deadline, even submission periods repeated over time. In addition, you need to understand if that call has a regular and defined launch frequency. It can vary or can not be defined in a precise manner. Even if you're late for the forthcoming deadline, you can already begin to initiate the process for the next deadline, overcoming in fact, a nasty habit of always doing things at the last minute.

You must also try to be **always informed on the call of interest**; sometimes there are extensions on deadlines of some calls, or the creation of bridge projects, a way to recover money already allocated for that specific action or area of intervention but unspent. It is advisable, therefore, to periodically monitor the reference sites, they may include published corrigendum, news and important updates, such as a change in the the expiration date.

The second fundamental information is the eligibility of the applicants. The calls indicate which organizations, public or private, can participate and therefore allow you to immediately check your eligibility.

Within the project it is possible to operate covering different organizational roles; Following there is **the terminology normally used in European projects**:

- ***Applicant / Coordinator***: the person who promotes, coordinates, calls the shots also from an administrative point. The Applicant has the legal responsibility for the project and signs the contract (*Grant Agreement*) with the European Commission. In some cases it is possible that the Applicant is different from the Coordinator: i.e. it is possible that the operational coordination is done by one partner, while the legal manager is another.
- ***Partners***: organizations that are officially part of the consortium of actuators of the project. They have an active role, receive part of the European financing and sign a partnership contract with the Applicant.
- ***Associated Partners***: organizations contributing to the implementation of the project, but do not benefit of the European contribution.

At this stage, therefore, you have to see what the call tells with respect to who may present the project and what are the requirements concerning the legal form. Finally you need to place this analysis within a broader reflection. In some cases, for example, we find a call you can not participate in directly, but you can propose it to other institutions, working with them for the presentation and implementation.

Satisfied that you can participate in the call, and that you are still in time to present a proposal, you must pay more attention to some important things. **Each call defines key priorities or exclusive lines and achievable implementation tool.** Or a call can define that projects are to deal with a certain issue or only certain types of intervention or specific services may be financed. This reflection helps you to understand if your project idea can find its place or if the call is suitable or not, thus enabling you to decide whether or not to proceed in the application.

Finally you have to **search for information about the intended recipients.** That means you must look in the call whether there are specific obligations with respect to the recipients of the project, knowing that there are broadly two possible types: the final recipients, even those beneficiaries, and intermediate recipients. The beneficiaries are the people targeted by the project, **the target group**, that is, those who have absolute priority over any action put in place; intermediate recipients are those persons who perform actions against the beneficiaries and that in turn are recipients of some project action. For example, in a vocational training project for young unemployed people, they are the ultimate beneficiaries, while the teachers who use the products of the project in their training activities are intermediate recipients.

Key words

Work Program Guides are often very long and elaborate and are usually available in English and French (sometimes also in German). So the ideal thing is to be able to quickly find key information using the index or search for keywords in the document.

The following table lists the main keywords in English:

Key Words (English)
Deadline
Conditions
Procedure
Eligible organisation
Who can apply
Number of participating organisations/minimum number of participating Countries
Eligible actions
Where to apply
How to apply
Application procedure
Funding rules
Maximum Grant
Available Budget
Award Criteria
Priorities
Guidelines, Guide for applicant
Application forms and Annexes

If you find the call or the funding program fit for you, the next step is to download and view the presentation materials of the project, including in particular:

- The form (***Application form***), i.e. the document to fill out to describe your project idea. Often the forms include questions followed by empty fields to fill out and may be in Word or editable PDF. Other times, the format is free and there is only a document indicating the content and page limits or characters for each field.

- The **guide for proposers** (***Guide for applicant***), which contains detailed information and tips on filling out the form and its contents.
- **Attachments** (***Annexes***) to the form: such as certificates of financial and legal identification (details in section 10.4)
- Information materials, guides for registration on the portals of the participants and online proposal submission (***online submission***). From 2014-2020 programming, in fact, the paper format has been eliminated entirely from the European project design for most of the funding programs.

10.2 Constraints to be taken into account

Each call sets constraints, limits on what you can ask and how to implement the project. Let's try to analyse them. We can say that the **economic constraints** are varied in nature, some related to the set of eligible projects and others specific for the realization of the single project.

Almost all the calls clearly define the **total amount of** economic **resources** available for the financing of projects that will be considered eligible; in many cases the internal divisions in the overall budget are also highlighted.

The division can also be related to the territorial areas. In other cases, the subdivision can be made for types of intervention or entities that can participate. But why should you lose yourself in the midst of a lot of numbers and figures not always easy to understand?

First of all, the reading of this data allows you to understand the extent of the funds available and as a consequence have a first idea about the orientation, by the financing authority, towards that type of project area. But this figure assumes a crucial importance particularly if associated with an additional element: **the maximum contribution that can be requested for each project**. In almost all cases, the call provides for a maximum amount to be requested and then available for the project. The total available amount (*budget available*) divided by the maximum quota that can be requested (*maximum grant*) allows you to understand how many projects, in the event that all proposals asked for maximum funding, could be financed.

On the basis of experience and some statistical calculations, on average between those who ask the most and those who ask lower amounts, you can assume the number of projects potentially eligible for subsidies. From this example, you understand the importance of this calculation, apparently a bit hard-working: this calculation allows you to assess whether it is appropriate to present a project in a call open to all European countries which is expected to finance at most, for example, 20 projects.

After this preliminary calculation you can analyse the economic constraints within the project. Almost all the calls provide, although with very different levels of detail to each other, the **constraints with respect to maximum eligible costs** for the individual budget headings. For example, there may be limits compared to the cost of certain benefits, certain types of expenditure can not exceed a certain percentage (e.g. the cost of subcontract may not exceed 30% of the total project cost), certain expenses are recognized only under certain conditions and so on, while some costs can not be fully recognized (e.g. purchase of computer / training equipment or renovation of buildings). It is important to verify these constraints before starting to write the budget in detail because some parameters may not be congruent with your project idea. Often, for example, one of the constraints relates to expenditure for the purchase, rental and renovation of real estate; if your idea is to renovate a building in order to realize a service, the call will not be appropriate and it would be useless to continue the design work.

Finally, another element, now present in almost all calls, is the "**co-financing**".

The term co-financing, introduced many years ago by the European projects and now present in many calls of private institutions and foundations, has a precise logic: the institution financing the project asks that the person who applies invests its own resources, financial and human. The percentage of co-financing required varies greatly from call to call, from the type of action financed and the geographical location of the project, ranging for example from 50% to 80%. But there are cases where funding covers 100% of the costs, as many actions of the macro- program Horizon 2020: often 100% is reserved for non-profit beneficiaries organizations.

The share of co-financing may be composed of various budget headings of the project, such as the cost of human resources involved in the project, the estimated cost resulting from the use of its facilities and resources (in kind payments, always consult the program because with few exceptions e.g., EuropeAid actions, contributions in kind are never admitted as co-financing), from their own financial resources or other project partners, from donations intended for this purpose by private sponsors and many more.

But economic constraints are not the only ones. You also have to analyse what the **time constraints** are placed by the call.

The maximum duration of the project is the first element that must be identified; calls often define a maximum time within which the project will be realized. Knowing this information allows you to understand if the time frame you had expected is consistent with the call and/or whether you can/must redefine other boundaries, perhaps by breaking down the project into sub-projects.

Another fact to be found, although not always expressed or placed in a clear and consistent way, is **the date by which the project must end**. In some cases, the end date is in relation to the actual start date of the project, coinciding with the moment of signing of the formal agreement between the Contracting Authority and the actuator of the project, while in other cases the date is independent or fixed a priori at a given time. This second mode is extremely problematic because often, because of bureaucratic delays in the approval and signing of the agreement, the project may start later than the start date set; this forces you to realize in compressed time planned actions in a completely different way.

Finally there are other small constraints to analyse.

Most of **the time the call has a specific mode of presentation, which must be respected, otherwise the project is not eligible**. Among these modes, we can mention the use of specially prepared forms and various required attachments as always listed in the reference call. Another preliminary constraint to take into account is the financial capacity of the aspirant *applicant*. For example, the aspiring *applicant* of "SME INSTRUMENT" action 1 *calls* must enter some data of its budget into a tool of financial analysis provided by the Commission:

https://ec.europa.eu/research/participants/urf/lfvSimulation.do.

If the outcome is positive, the person can proceed to run for *applicant*. If, instead, the result is negative, the same person can not submit a proposal as *applicant*. In that case the only alternatives are:

a) to give up the proposal;

b) cede the role of *applicant* to another person, if possible, given the nature and objectives of the call.
This preliminary check is in any case mandatory (except for a few cases), when for the Horizon 2020 program for example, the requested contribution is equal to or greater than € 500,000. Check out the rules and exceptions: http://ec.europa.eu/research/participants/docs/h2020-funding-guide/grants/applying-for-funding/register-an-organisation/financial-viability-self-check_en.htm.
Finally, it is worth **checking if special procedures subsequent to the project approval are explicitly provided**, such as the need to provide additional documentation or checks on the financial viability of the beneficiary, that the Financing Authority may request at any time. You do not know at this stage whether the project will be approved, but it is worth knowing what constraints to expect in the case of its realization.

10.3 In the shoes of those who will assess: the "application form trap"

What is the last step after finding that the call has a bearing on your idea, you have all the requirements to participate and you have carefully analysed all the constraints and limits imposed?
Often a part of the form asks to justify the project, to highlight what are the elements that make it necessary. In this regard you must then give, to justify your project, verifiable data, well-structured and complex readings of the reality and the phenomena that you want to address; **you must make as clear and "proved" as possible the reason of the need to accomplish the idea you have in mind.** There are not things in itself necessary or objectively valid.

Just to give some examples: an organization that promotes certain cultural themes can make sense in one area and have none in another; a project involving connection between people and assisted transport can be crucial in a rural area with poor or difficult communication systems but have no use in a urbanized environment. These are details that might escape you, because your representation of the world is linked to your history; these are variables to be taken into account, as could void your project if you were not able to make this representation understandable even to those who have a history different from yours.

A good way to see how your project is actually understandable in the eyes of third parties is to ask to a third person, expert on the subject, but not directly involved in the drafting process, to read it. It is better to receive criticism and negative judgments at this stage rather than in the assessment by the Commission.

It is very useful also to follow the instructions provided in the program guide and in the guide for applicant, which often provide details and suggestions about how to fill the various fields of the form.

Besides trying to make your project understandable to those who read and evaluate it, you should understand how, through which criteria and procedures, your work will be evaluated.

The **evaluation criteria** are always explained in more detail: in the call itself are included project evaluation tables listing the individual items that will be evaluated and the criteria by which the scores will be awarded. In other cases are defined areas which will be the subject of the evaluation and the general criteria with which they will be measured. In other cases, are defined the priorities and features on which the projects will be evaluated.

Then there is an infinite number of elements that are fundamental to the evaluation of the project. You must learn to highlight, and in some cases you could rightly say to "flush out", the elements that can make a difference in the approval of your project. Precisely for this reason there is a broad discussion on the kind of clarification of the criteria and methods of evaluation in project calls. The higher the detail, the greater the risk that projects are written only ad hoc for the evaluation criteria, enhancing the proliferation of the already extensive array of projects written just to get a loan, but behind which there is no substance. On the other hand, the less detail and clarification of the criteria, the greater the risk of subjective evaluation by the evaluators and the risk of possible misuse, leaving no possibility to check on what has been done during the assessment.

After you have selected and studied the documentation, once established that the call is right for you and taking into account all these aspects you can approach the last task: to define in detail the objectives and activities and complete the **form**.

The form has a logic aimed at evaluating, from third parties, and is organized on a collection of synthetic and quantitative describing data. From the point of view of the launcher of the call, which also has the task of evaluating the proposals, this approach is perfect and consistent:

1. It enables you to send the answers on what matters;
2. It allows homogenization of the expository method, making the analysis task faster and ensuring the possibility of comparison between the different projects presented;
3. In some cases, it also allows you to automate certain procedures through computerization of the form itself.

The logic is therefore not necessarily linked to the understanding and realization of the design process as a whole, but designed to highlight those aspects considered essential by those who set up the call.

So you have to figure out if and how the form allows you to express all the complexity and articulation of your project, in order to be able to make understandable what you have in mind through the use of this tool which is often mandatory. Sometimes you can also attach a detailed project, or additional documents, but do not rely on these additional materials to describe the true essence of your project, snubbing or incorrectly filling out the form, which is still the official project, so it has to be complete, clear and comprehensive.

Those with some experience know how limiting the forms often are: asking for content and aspects which seem irrelevant and neglecting others which are important to you, they are structured with a logic different from that which you would have designed and in most cases do not allow even that minimum of graphic diversification that allows to make it more readable. Despite this, you must learn to use this tool trying to take the most advantage possible, you must learn to navigate between frames, codes and summary diagrams without letting them destroy your creativity and the very nature of your project.

The forms, if misinterpreted as working tools, are likely to be real subtle traps.

The logical process, as has already been expressed, provides for the establishment of a project and then the compilation of a form. But how many actually do that? How many organizations have time and can afford the “luxury” or have the resources to follow these steps consistently? And how often do you learn about calls when it is too late? And how many times, taken from a thousand other "more important and more urgent" things, do you push it all back?

The form thus risks becoming the “grave” of thinking for projects. They place in sequence actions, names, phases, costs without trying to first build a comprehensive sense to include all the design thinking. In addition there is a further problem, absolutely not negligible: the project, if approved, must be planned and implemented; and sometimes you find yourself having to rethink everything because the logic of the form has nothing to do with reality.

These aspects should not discourage or confuse, because just from these risks, you must further develop the logic of the "project work".

The main elements that you can find within the form, obviously taking into account that this varies from program to program, can be listed as below:

- ❖ Presentation of partners and project coordinator
- ❖ Any priority to which the project refers
- ❖ Rationale or the overall logic of the project
- ❖ Innovation
- ❖ Aims
- ❖ Results
- ❖ Target group
- ❖ Definition of work packages and related deliverables
- ❖ Roles and responsibilities of partners
- ❖ Description of the activities from a time perspective
- ❖ Overall management in terms of management, dissemination, promotion and sustainability
- ❖ Budget

In the following links you can see the forms (application form) as an example.

(We recommend downloading the file to display properly

<table>
<tr><th>Program</th><th>Link for consultation</th></tr>
<tr><td>Erasmus Plus Action 1 Mobility</td><td rowspan="2">You can download the Erasmus+ application form from any National Agency web site. Here an example: http://www.erasmusplus.it/moduli-2/</td></tr>
<tr><td>Erasmus Plus Action 2 Strategic Partnerships</td></tr>
<tr><td>Horizon 2020</td><td>http://ec.europa.eu/research/participants/data/ref/h2020/call_ptef/pt/h2020-call-pt-ria-ia_en.pdf</td></tr>
</table>

10.4 Preliminary documents

The Concept Paper

The Concept Paper is a document that in short (MAX 3 pages) expresses the basic idea that gave birth to the project and how you will develop it. The concept paper must present the fundamentals and is primarily intended to organize a project partnership. The creator of the project, in fact, needs to create around himself a consortium that has clear the objectives of the proposal and the skills needed to bring it to fruition. The concept paper is placed during the project writing phase, prior to formally presenting the proposal to the financing authority.
There is no prescribed format of the Concept paper but there are elements that must be present in order to consider it an exhaustive document:

- ✓ *Organization Name*
- ✓ *Title of the proposed project*
- ✓ *Project content (no more than 300 words approximately)*
- ✓ *The "rationale", the basic problem / issue on which the project is based, (which must in turn have been deepened by a careful analysis of the needs and state of the art)*
- ✓ *The purpose of the project and its goals*
- ✓ *The strategy of the project / activities planned*
- ✓ *The expected results*
- ✓ *Innovation: how is the project different compared to the others? What is its innovative content?*
- ✓ *Features of the organization, expertise and skills*
- ✓ *Estimated budget*
- ✓ *Contact information*
- ✓ *Deadline by which the potential partner shall acknowledge with respect to the interest in participating in the project*

- ✓ *Deadline for submission of the proposal*
- ✓ *Any further clarification on the issues and topics addressed in the proposal (information supplied by footnotes page or attachments).*

Here we propose an example of the concept note

Program *XXXXX*
Specify the reference action for the project.

Idea
One or two sentences that summarize the project idea.
(E.g. The XX project aims to develop an innovative methodology for training operators in the footwear industry, in order to improve the competitiveness of European industry...).

Context / European relevance
Briefly explain why the project would be useful / necessary, which opportunity would be exploited. At this point you can also explain how the idea was born.

Aims
Describe the objectives of the action, you can divide the aims into general and specific objectives. In any case, if possible, try to be schematic (we recommend the use of bullet points)

Target group
Explain the target audience of the project: the final recipients, the public, the beneficiaries. In general, the needs identified in the previous section should be those of the target group.

Activity
Briefly explain what actions / activities you want to implement.

Indicate at this point, if you already know, the consortium partners, indicating the list of countries and organizations involved.

Expected results

Not to be confused with the objectives to which they are connected (E.g. If the goal is to improve the cultural offer in your city, an expected result might be the organization of a festival of contemporary art, which involves a large number of citizens and artists)

Resources

Making an estimate of the resources needed, also in principle, is essential. The term resources means: human, financial, equipment, subcontracting, etc.

Duration of the project

- ☐ 2 years
- ☐ 3 years

N.B. Do not exceed the number of three pages

The letter of support

The letter of support is a document written by the target group or the stakeholders of a project, useful to show their interest in the project development to develop and to be involved in it. The letter can be sent by the coordinator either at the time of proposal submission or at a later stage, to give strength to the *dissemination* or *exploitation* of the project results / products. It also represents an additional assurance that the project enjoys wide support and that the final recipients of the project results are already widely involved. These entities are also referred to as “silent partners” and would normally not receive a budget from the project support activities.
Below you can find a possible example of the Letter of support (keep in mind that there are no standard formats).

Example 1

To the project coordinator
for the
<Name of the project>

submitted as a project proposal within the *<Name of the programme>* of the European Commission
I the undersigned, confirm on behalf of my organization,________(please insert the name of your organization), our interest in the above mentioned project. We would like to be kept informed about the progress of this project and support the project submission.

<Name of the project> addresses issues critical to *<theme of the project>*, as yet not addressed elsewhere at a European level. We believe that *Name of the project* is in line with the goals and aspirations of *<Name of the organization>*, and is consistent with the strategies of our organization.
We therefore fully support this initiative and we confirm we would be glad to make further use of the project's results. We encourage the European Commission to fund this project and wish every success to the project Consortium and for the accomplishment of the proposed work.
This document does not have a legally binding character.

*Date,*_________
Stamp of the organization and signature of its representative

Example 2

To be printed on letterhead paper>

LETTER OF SUPPORT

Supporting Organisation:
Name of organisation: *<insert organisation name>*
Contact person: *<insert name>*, *<insert position>*
Address: *<insert address>*
Country: *<insert Country>*

I hereby declare the intention to support *<name of the coordinating organisation>* and their activities in the *<type of action>* consortium in order to realize the activities, project objectives and expected impacts of the project *<name of the project>*. For this goal, my organisation has the intention to provide its network, expertise and support during the project period and after, without any binding commitments.

____________________ ____________________

(Signature) (Stamp, if available)
<name>
<date>

The letter of intent

Depending on the Program, the letter of intent is planned either optionally or mandatorily when sending the project proposal; it is prepared by the partners to ensure mutual agreement about the actual taking of responsibility with respect to the project, and above all, in details covering activities to be carried out and the economic budget available. This documentation, which should be on the letterhead of the organization and to be sent to the coordinator, provides a brief description of the main lines of an agreement between one or

more parties on what to do and on the economic contribution expected from each party, before the contract is finalized. It is not a legally binding act, but it is a serious commitment of mutual involvement.
Here's an example:

MODEL LETTER OF INTENT/COMMITMENT FOR APPLICANT, PARTNERS
PARTICIPATING IN, AND/OR THIRD PARTIES PROVIDING A CASH CONTRIBUTION TO,
THE PROPOSED PROJECT.

This letter must be written on the official letterhead paper of the organisation.
Call for proposals VP/2009/011
Letter of intent commitment *[delete as appropriate]*

This letter is to confirm that *(name of applicant, partner or third party organisation)*, represented by *(name of legal representative)* is intending/committed *[delete as appropriate]* to participate in and/or contribute to the financing of *[delete as appropriate]* the project entitled *(title of project)*.

In terms of contribution to the costs of the project, *(name of applicant, partner or third party organisation)* intends to *[delete as appropriate*] provide a cash contribution to the project of ________ euros.

As a partner in this project, my organisation is undertaking to perform the following roles and tasks as set out in the work programme *(description of the roles and tasks): [to be filled in by project partners only]*
Date, place & legal representative's signature

The Mandate

The Mandate that many programs require as mandatory when sending the project proposal is prepared by the partners that give precisely mandate to the *applicant* to act in the name and on behalf of the other components of the proposal towards the funding authority for everything related to the contacts and communications during evaluation and the possible *grant agreement* contracting in case of approval. It is therefore a legally binding act. Where required, the funding authority provides the outline to be used which can then be filled with the data specific to each partner.

The Declaration of Honour

The Declaration of Honour is a statement used in all funding programs relating to formal eligibility of the *applicant*. By signing the Declaration of Honor the subject, in fact, states that:

- All information contained in the application form are correct
- The representative organization has financial and operational capacity to complete what the action or the work program proposes

It also certifies:

- Not being in bankrupt or being wound up, not being administered by the court which has not concluded an agreement with creditors, has not suspended its activities, it is not the subject of proceedings concerning those matters, or is in any analogous situation arising from a similar procedure planned by national laws and regulations
- It has not been tried for offenses relating to its professional activities
- It is not guilty of serious professional misconduct

- Meets its obligations regarding payment of taxes and contributions on work in accordance with the legislation governing its own country
- It is not subject to an administrative penalty referred to in Article 109(1) Financial Rules (Council Regulation 966/2012)

Finally, it recognizes that it is not in a position of conflict of interest of any kind with organizations managing the procedures for the award of funding.

10.5 How to present the technical and financial capacity if requested by the call

During the signing of the loan agreement, it is important that the European Commission, in programs that provide for it and in the case considered appropriate, estimate the actual existence of the following requirements: operational capacity and financial capacity.

Operational capacity:

This refers to the fact that proposing organizations should comply with the requirements and have the appropriate professional skills to carry out the proposed activities.

To this end, each proposer or only the coordinator may be required to present:

- An activity report covering the past two years
- The curriculum vitae of the person or persons responsible for the overall coordination / implementation of the proposed action on behalf of each organization involved or for the implementation of the work program of the organization (maximum four pages per curriculum vitae).

Normally this information is most often provided by completing the appropriate section of the Application Form during the writing of the project proposal.

Financial capacity

This refers to the fact that organizations must demonstrate that they have stable and sufficient financial resources to support the proposed activities, and to participate in their funding.

In this framework, two cases can typically occur:

- The first (usually in Programs relating to culture, education) concerns the coordinator to which may be requested: 1) the financial identification form duly completed and certified by the bank (original signatures required) that certifies the existence of a relationship of the current account with a bank in the country where the applicant resides; 2) the form concerning the financial capacity. This module requires you to send certain values reflected in the balance sheet of the *applicant* that will be used by the Financing Authority for calculating indices needed to understand the state of solvency, and finally the "health" of the financial beneficiary. This control is normally conducted after approval of the proposal. The timing, however, could potentially cause problems to the beneficiary which in absolute good faith could have participated in a call, be the winner and only after approval may be asked to prove to the financing Authority its "financial capacity". In that case, there may be two consequences:
  - 1. The financing authority requires to the primary beneficiary the activation of an insurance or bank before signing the grant agreement.

- 2. The beneficiary must give the role of *applicant* (as contractual interface and financial guarantor in respect of funding authority) to another partner of the group with better financial rating.

- In research and innovation programs, primarily the example of Horizon 2020, however, depending on the call and / or the amount of the contribution requested, the aspiring applicant must calculate its financial health by using a tool available and set by the Commission. Only if the result is positive, the entity can continue with the role of *applicant* in the application. See section 10.2 for further details

10.6 Online registration and PIC number

What is the Participant Identification Number (PIC)

What is the Participant Identification Number (PIC)

A unique identifier called PIC, Participant Identification Code is assigned to all organizations participating in funding programs managed by the European Commission (research, innovation and development, culture, education etc.). The PIC is used by the organization for presentation and subsequent management in the event of approval of each of its proposals. The main advantage of this identification tool is to simplify the administrative processes related for example to the presentation of the proposal. Thanks to the PIC every organization has in its "personal area" of the Participant Portal the obligation to upload a number of administrative documents, according to its legal nature. Once loaded, these documents will no longer be attached, the EC picks them up automatically by any entity involved in a project. If your organization has previously participated in the 7th Framework Programme (or other European funding programs), it is likely that it already has a PIC. During the process of creating (or after updating the data at the time put into the system), there are different subjects for different tasks and responsibilities. At least two are the subjects usually involved:

- The contact person who will be the person contacted for issues related to the operating use of the PIC
- The LEAR (Legal Entity Appointed Representative) organization is the one who creates, preserves and communicates, who is responsible, the PIC, and is accountable to the European Commission.

How to create the PIC

The steps to get the PIC are:

1- You must first create an account in the **authentication system of the European Commission (ECAS or European Commission Authentication System)** https://webgate.ec.europa.eu/cas/eim/external/register.cgi.

2- The PIC is provided at the end of the registration process and can be used to submit proposals after 48 hours. During registration, the URF (Unique Registration Facility), the office that handles and processes requests does not check any duplicate records; this will be done only if your proposal is accepted. In case of double registration, the PIC will be modified and the user will be informed at the start of contracting.

3- Once you have registered, you can access the **Participant Portal, for the program in which you want to participate,** and the services it offers, such as the URF service that allows you to obtain the code: http://ec.europa.eu/research/participants/portal/desktop/en/organisations/register.html

4- In order to make the registration completely effective it is necessary to provide, in the page of your organization, some documents that are used to test and certify your legal and financial status. The type of documents varies depending on the program and the legal nature of the organization, but the main ones are:
5- Legal entity form: http://ec.europa.eu/budget/contracts_grants/info_contracts/legal_entities/legal_entities_en.cfm#it
6- Financial Identification form: http://ec.europa.eu/budget/contracts_grants/info_contracts/financial_id/financial_id_en.cfm#it

Both documents require you to attach documents in support of the forms, proof of the data declared and signed.

The Participant Portal is the access point for management and electronic communication with the European Commission, made available to all potential interested parties. The portal hosts all the services, the necessary documents, forms, calls, and the most relevant news on the topic. In the personal area, accessible through the PIC, you can also follow the project in its lifecycle. Right now there are two platforms, one for the management of research projects that refers to DG Research and Innovation; the second refers to the actions managed by the EACEA Executive Agency.

Some of the programs operated by the former are:

- Horizon 2020
- Research Fund for Coal & Steel
- COSME
- 3rd Health Programme
- Consumer Programme
- FP7 & CIP Programmes (2007-2013)

For a more comprehensive list of all programs in the platform you can see the following link:

http://ec.europa.eu/research/participants/portal/desktop/en/opportunities/other/index.html.

Some of the programs managed by the second platform are:

- Creative Europe
- Erasmus Plus
- Europe for Citizens
- EU Aid Volunteers.

For each reference:
http://ec.europa.eu/education/participants/portal/desktop/en/home.html

10.7 How to carry out the procedures of certification of expenditure

There are some programs that entails high grant rates (think about *TEN-T* for network infrastructure and connection, *Interreg* for trans-border cooperation, COSME for Competitiveness and Innovation). The experience of the previous multiannual financial frameworks highlighted that many sources of error in the reporting of projects relate to personnel costs and indirect costs, often calculated using a method that does not respect the provisions of the loan agreement.

Therefore, considering for example the current program for Research and Innovation Horizon 2020 if the grant requested is greater than or equal to the amount of € 325,000, in the final phase of the project during which you present to the Commission the "Final Report", it is required that the project report certification through an audit certificate CFS (*certificate on financial statement*).

The certificate is an independent report produced by an auditor who supports the request for reimbursement of project expenses incurred and reported under the European funding contract. The independent audit is designed to express an opinion on compliance with the rules laid down in the Grant Agreement and, in particular, the objectives of the auditor will focus on eligibility requirements and eligibility verification that the project costs are actually incurred, that were necessary for carrying out the project activities, that are proven and incurred for the period stipulated in the contract. The general scheme of the Certificate that is fixed and can not be changed is contained in the annex 5 of the Grant Agreement. It is good to know, however, that the beneficiary is solely responsible for the final report and that the presence of an external audit does not prevent the Commission from carrying out checks on the certified costs or activating the auditors of the European Court for further investigation.

Each beneficiary is free to choose any qualified external auditor, provided that both the following **conditions** are met:

- the external auditor must be an agency independent from the beneficiary;
- the external auditor must be qualified in accordance with Directive 2006/43/EC of the European Parliament and Directives 78/660/EEC, 83/349/EEC, 84/253/EEC of the European Council. For Italy, in practice can perform the task those who are enrolled in the Register of Auditors, established by Decree No. 88/1992 at the Ministry of Justice.

Some practical advice for beneficiaries and the reference documents

An example of guidance to the financial aspects relating to the Horizon 2020 program is available at the following link:
http://ec.europa.eu/research/participants/data/ref/h2020/grants_manual/lev/h2020-guide-lev_en.pdf

- Certification Support Notes provided by the Commission itself:

http://ec.europa.eu/research/participants/data/ref/fp7/89531/guidelines-audit-certification_en.pdf

- All information regarding the CFS are available at:

http://ec.europa.eu/research/participants/docs/h2020-funding-guide/grants/grant-management/checks-audits-reviews-investigations_en.htm

Useful tips :

- Pay attention to the information and methods used in the administrative/accounting practice of a beneficiary/applicant for a grant within the Horizon 2020 program, especially with regard to the calculation of personnel costs. In fact, following a grant application equal or greater than €325,000, to avoid the risk of being cut off part of the loan, you should always be able to provide a CFS to certify that you conform to the methods of calculation of direct costs provided by the program.
- Make sure that the external auditor chosen to produce the CFS is not linked to the beneficiary in any way, making sure therefore of the absence of conflicts of interest. Also, check whether the auditor has the qualifications required by national legislation (as implemented by Directive 2014/56/EU or other following act) on statutory audits of annual accounts and consolidated accounts.
- Register on the portal of the participants well in advance of the date of expiry of the call and make sure that all the other partners have done the same thing and that all have the PIC. This would avoid the unpleasant consequences of technical problems of the portal or other obstacles that could compromise the correct and timely submission of the proposal.

- An example of Grant Agreement related to the new program for research and innovation (2014-2020) Horizon 2020 is available at the following link:

http://ec.europa.eu/research/participants/data/ref/h2020/mga/gga/h2020-mga-gga-multi_en.pdf

In the same document it has provided a model of the certificate on the financial statements to be issued by the external auditor (Annex 5).

- Wherever possible, produce and send in a pre-approval *Certificate on the methodology for calculating the unit costs*; in practice you require an external auditor to issue a report about:
  - ✓ the analytical accounting practices used
  - ✓ the accounting methodology in place for the calculation of the unit costs, in particular for personnel and indirect costs.

Once (if) obtained, the approval from the Commission protects from future objections (and potential budget cuts) regarding the methodology used for reporting project costs.
All the details at this link:
http://ec.europa.eu/research/participants/docs/h2020-funding-guide/grants/applying-for-funding/register-an-organisation/certifications_en.htm

11. Project proposal process and award criteria

The evaluation process can be understood as a path of knowledge aimed at making a judgment. This cognitive step will have to be practised intentionally and clarified if you want to manage the project. You need to consider two types of "evaluation": the first is internal to the project team, while the second one concerns the formal process for evaluating proposals. One can not ignore the other, because implementing internal evaluation, from the beginning of the design, allows you to respect those evaluation criteria expressed in the call and that external evaluators themselves will closely consider during formal assessment.

Internal evaluation, made by the project team, helps to consider the different profiles of the project: financial, administrative, ethical; this can be accomplished mainly in three different phases:

- **Before you start the design phase itself**, trying to understand its impact and if there are the organizational, political, economic conditions to support the project;
- **During the design**, in order to check that the project is translated in respect of what had been expected and to plan any corrective steps;
- **After the design completion**, as operation of second reading of the entire project and check of the achievement of objectives and results declared in the project.

The assessment, when shared, becomes a valuable opportunity for exchange, a reflection that leads to the growth of the organization, the workers, the volunteers and the implemented intervention.

After having decided that the call is relevant to your idea, you have all the requirements to participate and you have carefully analysed all the constraints and limits imposed by the call, **you must understand what criteria will be used for project evaluation.**

A first overall focus is just to **not take anything for granted**. Too often when you write a project you take for granted many things that you will find are decisive for its evaluation. You should apply the same rule used when you write any other text: do not assume that what you think is what others think, that what you know is also known by others, that what you write it is also clear to the reader. And you know how difficult it is; it means somehow to come out of yourself to put yourself in the shoes of someone else that, in the particular case of the project's evaluation, we do not know who he is, which level of familiarity he has with what we are dealing with and which is his orientation on the issue.

With variations depending on the specific programs, the European Commission identifies the following issues on which the assessor is required to make a judgment:

- Relevance of the proposal
- Quality of work scheduling
- Innovative nature of the project
- Quality of the Consortium
- European added value
- Cost-benefit analysis
- Impact
- Quality of the exploitation plan (dissemination and exploitation of results)

The following table shows an example, relating to the Erasmus Plus - Strategic Partnership, of the projects evaluation criteria, with their scoring.

Relevance of the project (maximum 30 points)	**1** The relevance of the proposal to: - the objectives and the priorities of the Action **2** The extent to which: - the proposal is based on a genuine and adequate needs analysis; - the objectives are clearly defined, realistic and address issues relevant to the participating organisations and target groups; - the proposal is suitable of realising synergies between different fields of education, training and youth; - the proposal is innovative and/or complementary to other initiatives already carried out by the participating organisations; - the proposal brings added value at EU level through results that would not be attained by activities carried out in a single country.
Quality of the project design and implementat ion (maximum 20 points)	- The **clarity, completeness and quality of the work programme**, including appropriate phases for preparation, implementation, monitoring, evaluation and dissemination; - The **consistency between project objectives and activities proposed**; - The **quality and feasibility** of the methodology proposed; - The existence and relevance of **quality control measures** to ensure that the project implementation is of high quality, completed in time and on budget; - The extent to which **the project is cost-**

	effective and allocates appropriate resources to each activity. -
Quality of the project team and the cooperation arrangements (maximum 20 points)	1. The extent to which: - the project involves **an appropriate mix of** complementary **participating organisations** with the necessary profile, experience and expertise to successfully deliver all aspects of the project; - the **distribution of responsibilities and tasks** demonstrates the commitment and active contribution of all participating organisations; - if relevant for the project type, the project involves **participation of organisations from different fields** of education, training, youth and other socio-economic sectors; - the project involves newcomers to the Action. 2. **The existence of effective mechanisms for coordination and communication** between the participating organisations, as well as with other relevant stakeholders. 3. If applicable, the extent to which the involvement of a participating organisation from a Partner Country brings an essential added value to the project (if this condition is not fulfilled, the project will not be considered for selection).
Impact and dissemination (maximum 30 points)	1. The **quality of measures for evaluating** the outcomes of the project 2. The potential impact of the project: - on participants and participating

	organisations, during and after the project lifetime; - outside the organisations and individuals directly participating in the project, at local, regional, national and/or European levels. 3. The **quality of the dissemination plan**: the appropriateness and quality of measures aimed at sharing the outcomes of the project within and outside the participating organisations. 4. If relevant, the extent to which the proposal describes how the materials, documents and media produced will be made freely available and promoted through open licences, and does not contain disproportionate limitations. 5. The **quality of the plans for ensuring the sustainability of the project**: its capacity to continue having an impact and producing results after the EU grant has been used up.

The following table[10] shows instead the evaluation criteria of the Horizon 2020 program. It should be noticed how in this case the criteria have been reduced to 3, although then split into sub-criteria that have to be studied carefully.
The table also informs you about the criteria applicable to all types of action of the program but also about further criteria that are added according to this or that specific action.

[10] http://ec.europa.eu/research/participants/data/ref/h2020/wp/2014_2015/annexes/h2020-wp1415-annex-ga_en.pdf

Type of action	Excellence	Impact	Quality and efficiency of the implementation
All types of action	The following aspects will be taken into account, to the extent that the proposed work corresponds to the topic description in the *Work Programme*	The extent to which the outputs of the project would contribute at European and/or international level.	The following aspects will be taken into account:
All types of action	Clarity and pertinence of the objectives; Credibility of the proposed methodology;	The expected impacts as mentioned in the work programme under the relevant topic	Consistency and effectiveness of the work plan, including the appropriateness of allocation of resources and tasks; Complementarity of the participants in the consortium (where relevant); Appropriateness of the management structures and procedures, including risk and innovation management.

Type of action	Excellence	Impact
Research and innovation; Innovation; SME instrument	Effectiveness of the concept, including interdisciplinarity, where relevant; Extent that the proposed work is beyond the state of the art, and demonstrates innovation potential (e.g. ground-breaking objectives, novel concepts and approaches)	Enhance innovation capacity and integration with new knowledge; Strengthen competitiveness and growth of companies, developing the meeting between innovation and European and global market needs; where relevant, bringing these innovations into the market; Any other social and environmental impact (not addressed before); Effectiveness of the proposed action to disseminate and exploit the project results (including Intellectual Property Right management), to communicate the project and manage data research where relevant.

Type of action	Excellence	Impact
Coordination & support actions	Effectiveness of the concept; Quality of the proposed coordination and/or support measures	Effectiveness of the proposed action to disseminate and exploit the project results (including Intellectual Property Right management), to communicate the project and manage data research where relevant.

Type of action	**Excellence**	**Impact**
ERA-NET	Level of ambition in the collaboration and commitment of the participants in the proposed ERA-NET action to pool national resources and coordinate their national/regional research programmes	Achievement of critical mass for the funding of trans-national projects by pooling of national/regional resources and contribution to establishing and strengthening a durable cooperation between the partners and research programmes; Effectiveness of the proposed action to disseminate and exploit the project results

Type of action	Excellence	Impact
Pre-commercial procurement Cofund actions Public procurement of innovative solutions	Progress beyond the state of the art in terms of the degree of innovation needed to satisfy the procurement need	Strengthening the competitiveness and growth of companies by developing innovations meeting the needs of European and global procurement markets; Effectiveness of the proposed action to disseminate and exploit the project results (including Intellectual Property Right management), to communicate the project More forward-looking concerted procurement approaches that reduce fragmentation of demand for innovative solutions

The technical evaluation process

The process of evaluation of proposals, after having verified the eligibility requirements, is given to 2 or 3 experts, selected on the basis of what is described in the next point, who individually shall consider the proposal and assess it according to the criteria set in the table above. After an individual evaluation, experts will gather for a "Consensus meeting" during which they compare, and review their assessments in the light of those of colleagues and come to a common "Consensus Report", where are collected scores, comments and recommendations for the Commission. The proposals that have received a higher vote, following the rank list, access the possibility of receiving funding, until depletion of funds previously allocated.

The tasks of the evaluators And how to become an "expert"

The so-called "experts" are considered peer reviewers who assist the Commission mainly in two ways:

- Evaluation of proposals
- Project monitoring

In addition, experts may be called for the preparation, implementation and evaluation of programs and design of policies. To the experts are mainly assigned assessment tasks within the Horizon 2020 program, inherent excellence in science, technology and innovation. In addition, experts can apply to become "business innovation coaches", a kind of mentors, to support those projects funded under the dedicated instrument for SMEs. The selection of experts is made on the basis of the curriculum and past experiences, prior application through the Portal of the Participants. The call for applications was launched in 2013, at the advent of the new Horizon program and will be in force until its closure in 2020. The same selection procedure is also applied to those who want to run for experts for the programs managed by EACEA.

Experts therefore generally have a high level of experience in one of the areas of the program. Upon registration in the Portal of the Participants, in fact, experts must indicate the area or areas in which they have more proven experience. On this basis, they are chosen and assigned to the evaluation of projects addressing the scope of their expertise.

The evaluation process requires the experts to consider the projects by comparing them with published criteria, by assigning scores, comments and recommendations to the Commission. Monitoring, however, consists of assisting the project officer of the Commission, overseeing the progress of ongoing projects. The involvement of experts in the creation of policies and the evaluation of programs, finally, requires less technical support. The experts are required to assess the implementation and the results of programs at a more strategic level.

Evaluators are required to be available about 10 days a year and receive a refund for the time spent in their activities, meals and accommodation depending on how many days have been involved.
All information on the processes of evaluation, nomination and selection of experts, can be found at:
http://ec.europa.eu/research/participants/portal/desktop/en/experts/index.html

Useful tips:

- Always put in place an evaluation of your project, internal to the project team;
- Understand what are the criteria by which your project will be assessed;
- Do not take anything for granted when arguing your project idea;
- When you write "go out of yourself" and put yourself in the shoes of those who evaluate;
- Demonstrate clearly why it is needed to realize your project idea;
- Arrange for a third person to read your project proposal;
- Try to find the elements that make the difference;
- Try to measure out the details;
- When writing the project, at the end of each section, re-read what you wrote comparing it with the criteria of evaluation and correct if what you produce is not in line with the standards.

11.1 Strategy in case of non-approval

During the design, it can happen that months of work of conception and writing of a project, could resolve in an (apparent) stalemate because the proposal, at the end of the selection, was not admitted to financing, and this is not because of a formality or a technical problem, but an evaluation that considered the proposal qualitatively unsatisfactory.

Do not despair: not all proposals can be considered worthy of funding, although good, and the time spent writing is actually a job from which you can still capitalize on experience and learn important elements for improvement.

The first, and certainly the most important opportunity for reflection is offered by the European Commission, the same one that has rejected the proposal. **All projects, in fact, are read by at least two external evaluators on the basis of the various parameters and the written report of their evaluation is sent to the creator of the project.** This is a very important chance to understand what were the strengths and weaknesses of the project, where then you can be reasonably confident that, if you fill the gaps, the project may be more likely to be eligible for funding on the next attempt.

Other helpful tips to make sure that the next time the probability that the "target" is centred increases:

- Monitor publications, initiatives and web communications promoted or participated in by the European Commission or the National Agency in the topic of interest (education, environment, research, culture,...). In this way you can catch the policies and feelings that drive Europe to be able to produce, through a proposed project, the **European added value** that is required in the proposals, as we have seen in the various aspects covered by the evaluation.
- Knowing to adapt your proposal to the programming period and the policies in place at the social, cultural and political level ("become attached" to a project can make you lose sight of the need to integrate the proposals with the needs, feelings, thematic priorities or sector that the European Union rides or promotes at that particular historic moment).
- Participate in workshops, info-days and events organized by the European Commission or the National Agency: a lot of information or ideas for

improvement come from just such events. Listening, talking and seeing for yourself, allows you to understand many more nuances and create that networking crucial in developing or reviewing a proposal.

Useful tips:

Before reviewing the proposal, carefully re-read the Commission's or the National Agency's evaluation. Try to:

- Analyse the negative reviews and try to change those parts of the project, making them the strengths of the new project;
- Try to enrich your idea, depending on updates of the sector from year to year.

SECTION 3 IMPLEMENTATION OF A EUROPEAN PROJECT

12. Contractual aspects

From the formal point of view, the implementation of an approved project begins with the signing of contracts, namely:

- the contract with the European Commission or its delegated agencies centralized or decentralized, also called Grant Agreement;
- the Consortium Agreement, i.e. the contract between the organizations participating in the project so that they govern their internal relations;
- any subcontracts or contracts for the supply of goods and / or services necessary to the implementation of one or more phases of the project.

In this chapter these types of contracts will be analysed, highlighting the various rights and obligations of the parties.

12.1 The contract with the Commission

The agreement between the European Commission and the candidate selected for the grant is called the **grant agreement. The contract with the Commission sets out the rights and obligations of the participants, the financial rules and in particular the provisions for:**

1. **the achievement of its objectives**
2. **changes in the composition of the consortium**
3. **the payment of the European financial contribution**
4. **the conditions for eligibility of any necessary expenditure, as well as rules for dissemination and exploitation.**

The contract between the Commission (or the National Agency) and all participants in an action is concluded by the signing by the Commission and the coordinator. The candidate requesting the grant that has been selected, assumes the role of **beneficiary** once the agreement has been signed. The other participants identified in the contract participate according to the rules included and enjoy the rights and obligations of participants. Any participant joining the contract becomes the owner, towards the Union, of the rights and obligations of participants.

A project begins after the signing of the grant agreement and continues with the implementation of the work program. The grant agreement also indicates the period of eligibility of the project activities, the maximum European contribution to the project costs, as well as the co-financing mechanism that will be applied.

The contract establishes the rights and obligations of all participants. All contracts are based on a standard contract that is structured as follows:

- Contract model fixing the composition and evolution of the consortium, the entry into force and the duration of the project, the European contribution, how to report payments and special clauses;
- General description of the work;
- General Conditions: project implementation, financial information and intellectual property rights.

For any modification of the consortium, which takes place during the project, the contract will have to be formally amended.

The body of the contract is signed by the Commission and by the Coordinator of the project and contains the essential elements of the project, such as the duration, the starting date, the amount of financing, payment terms, deadlines for payments, reporting and delivery of reports, as well as the rules on the law applicable to the contract and procedures concerning cases of disputes between participants. The body of

the contract can be amended or supplemented in some standards, such as the reporting method, by inserting some clauses, referred to as "*special clauses*", indicated in a list published by the Commission.
In the grant agreement, there is also a specific provision that indicates how long, after the conclusion of the project, records and documents related to the project activities must be kept by the coordinator, who must make them available at any time to the Commission, which reserves the right to carry out checks and controls even after the end of the project. Upon termination of the Agreement, the Commission (or the National Agency) may decide to terminate the relationship, without giving any compensation. Another scenario that leads to disruption of the contractual relationship is when the beneficiary fails in the realization of fundamental obligations that fall on it in accordance with the provisions of the grant agreement, also including its annexes.

12.2 The Consortium Agreement

The Consortium Agreement (CA) is the agreement that governs relations between the Coordinator/Applicant and project partners. It must be signed by all partner organizations of a project to provide reasonable assurance that the project action will be implemented in accordance with the provisions of the grant agreement. Its purpose is to regulate some problems and issues that may arise during the lifetime of the project, such as the form of cooperation, financial provisions and intellectual property rights. The European Commission is not part of the agreement and has no role in the choice of the parties, the terms to be considered appropriate to the nature and purpose of the partnership and the interests considered. This document is highly recommended for all projects and it is expected that it will be signed after the grant agreement.

Checklist of the matters that must be settled in CA:

GENERAL INFORMATION

- *Identification of the parties* - In the Consortium Agreement must be specified the benchmark contract with the Commission, the list of partners with the indication of the legal representative and the head office. It should be ensured in particular that the signatories of the CA have the authority to commit the organization to which they belong. This check should be extended to the powers of those representing the partners.

List of staff members - The EC advises to indicate the names of those who will work on the project especially to strengthen the obligation of secrecy. This indication is also useful at the time of reporting staff costs.

Third parties that provide resources - If you use the resources of third parties, you should indicate the type and the use made of it. Also in this case it is better to indicate the relative information in an annex.

PREAMBLE

Reasons for signing the agreement - The CA should contain a description of the activities carried out prior to the signing of the contract with the EC. One reason for this description is that it is appropriate to link the partners to statements made before the contract is signed, in order to enforce the so-called "pre-contractual liability".

Definition of terms used - The checklist requires that the expressions used in the CA are defined. It is recommended to define only expressions whose meaning is not contained in the agreement with the EC or in the legal sources.

OBJECT

Activities to be carried out - The object of the CA is the specification of the obligations and rights of the participants on the contents of the contract with the EC.

Beginning and duration of effectiveness - The date of the commencement and conclusion of the CA should be indicated. As mentioned in the introduction, it is appropriate that the CA or at least its preliminary enter into force already in the drafting of the proposal. The CA, although preceded by a preliminary, should last longer than the duration of the contract with the EC. Indeed, in it are regulated subjects, such as those concerning the secrecy and industrial property rights which have a bearing even after the end of the contract with the EC.

TECHNICAL REGULATIONS

Technical contribution of the parties - Precise definition of the activities and links between the activities of the partners.

Technical resources made available - human resources, equipment, information (location, language, etc.).

Limits of technical effort - limits of resources commitment should not be based on results, but in terms of quantity of commitment

Procedure for amendments

Rules in case of non-compliance

ORGANIZATIONAL RULES

Governing bodies (decision-making, administrative, technical) - The CA is a contract with a term, multi-person and with communal aims. Among the most important consequences of these characteristics is the identification of who takes the common decisions, throughout the duration of the contract. Usually decisions are entrusted to bodies composed of representatives of the partners. A clear definition of the governing bodies, their functions, composition, operation will allow an agile management. Usually they can be divided into decision-making, managerial, technical and advisory bodies.

The presence of all these organs is optional and depends on the size and type of projects.

Coordination of the organs - If there are more bodies, it is appropriate to introduce coordination instruments.

Changes of the Agreement - It is necessary to establish rules for the amendment of the various provisions of the CA. An important role in this regard could be performed by the decision-making body.

FINANCIAL RULES

Financial Plan - Detailed estimates of costs, allocation of the European contribution, financing provided by third parties, budget and forms (it is useful to submit with the CA a document that establishes the distribution of funding among partners and the payment schedule).

Payments - Common expenditure, method of payment, terms, currency, payment costs, taxes, interest, identification of the management costs.

Expenses Audit - Reporting methods and control of expenditure and audit certification; it is appropriate to set uniform rules for reporting and certification.

RULES ON INTELLECTUAL AND INDUSTRIAL PROPERTY

Privacy - Obligation limits: information already known, public and belonging to third parties.

Ownership of the results, common property and problematic cases - The checklist recommends to dictate rules in more problematic cases, such as the one in which the produced knowledge belongs to multiple partners. It is useful in this regard to establish rules of exploitation, such as for example, a breakdown by territories.

Access - Rules for access: object, limitations and fees.

Protection of results – it is necessary to determine who is protecting the project results.

Exploitation - Rules should be provided for the commercial exploitation of the results.

Dissemination and publication - It might be remembered that the publication of information concerning the project must specify that it has been realized with the contribution of the Commission and that it is not responsible for the use made by third parties of information concerning the project. The publication ban could be extended beyond the expiry of the contract, if the dissemination of knowledge has a negative impact on its protection.

Sub-licences and Pre-existing Know-how excluded by the contract - It is important to establish what knowledge pre-existing to the project are used in the project and which are excluded from other partners' access.

LEGAL RULES

Legal form - Which legal form is given to the CA.

End of contract and contractual penalties.

Applicable law and competent court - National law and private codifications.

Staff transfer - The checklist provides that, in case of the occurrence of the staff transfer from one partner to another, the rules of that transfer should be specified.

Signature of the contract - The CA has to be signed by those who represent negotiating partners. The checklist requires that the addresses are provided for communication between partners.

Final Clauses - The CA contains several clauses that close the text and that are often features of international contracts, e.g.: *Entire agreement* (with this clause it is stated that the CA supersedes all other agreements hitherto taken), Severability *Clause* (if one or more clauses are invalid, however, the CA is valid regarding the remaining clauses), *Counterparts* (you determine the number of copies in which is written the CA), *Assignment* (it prohibits the transfer to third parties of the obligations arising from CA).

12.3 The Subcontracting

This is the contract made by a project participant with a third party (subcontractor), for the execution of activities in the framework of the project. As a rule, participation in a project as a subcontractor does not allow the recognition of property rights on the results. The Grant Agreement takes into account employees, contractors, suppliers of goods and services and affiliates. The general rules are: prohibition to commit contrary to the contract, exclusion of any claims against the Commission, extension of the obligations of the contracting parties to the third party (controls of the Commission and the Court of Accounts, notification to the Commission of data necessary for the evaluation, information to be provided to Member States or Associated States, compliance with the reporting procedures and authorization for the Commission to publish some data on beneficiaries, processing of personal data, rules on eligibility of costs, audit and financial controls), compliance with the principles on the subject of public contracts (motivation, transparency, equal treatment and prohibition of conflict of interest).

The beneficiary may use resources that are made available by a third party to carry out its part of the work in two ways:

1) Third parties provide resources for the beneficiaries;
2) The third party carries out part of the project.

In the first case the hypotheses are:

- Subjects that use collective resources of their members;
- Other cases, such as a research institute that conducts its research with a graduate of a university.

In the second case the hypotheses are:

- Collective subjects (associations, companies, consortia);
- Affiliates or third parties subject to control, in fact or in law, direct or indirect, of a beneficiary or that are subject to the same checks of beneficiaries.

The calls indicate the maximum percentage of budget or activities that can be assigned to external subcontractors to the consortium, as it assumes that the partners have the necessary skills to implement the project within their organizations. You usually resort to subcontracting for very specific, *one-off* and / or highly technical activities, such as the development of a website or communication materials, but subcontractors can not be responsible for the results of the project.

12.4 The responsibility of the Coordinator

The responsibility of the coordinator deserves a special note. In general terms, the coordinator is responsible for the overall management of the project. This position is usually held by that organization or institution (usually coinciding with the *applicant*, i.e. the entity that has formally submitted the proposal) which in legal terms is identified as receiving the grant from the European Commission. In terms of definition, **the coordinator is the one which plays the role of agent (with representation) of other contracting parties with regard to the European Commission, which commissioned**

the co-financed activity. It is, in other words, the only interface between all the applicants and the European Commission.

Typically, the coordinator is also the *team leader*, that is the *primus inter pares* among the partners involved in the project, which assumes, however, a co-ordinating role. Having the responsibility of coordinating the project means managing the activities, so as to ensure their smooth implementation for the realization of goals and objectives. The coordinator is in fact responsible for defining the tasks and the work to be assigned to each project partner, manages the program and the timing on the implementation of activities and is responsible for internal communication between the partners and external with all relevant stakeholders, thus ensuring the quality of products and project results. Sometimes, the coordinator - distinguishing itself in this way from the *team leader* - plays only an administrative function which may go so far as to realize an organization activity of the existing *networking*. It therefore:

1. will handle the transmission of information on current activities of the various partners to the European Commission;
2. will collect contributions from the EU and distribute them to the partners;
3. will take care of the accounting of expenses incurred;
4. will check the fulfilment of the duties of partners.

The coordinator, as an agent, has the obligation to represent each project partner in the relationship with the customer. Technically, the mandate given to the coordinator "is special, with representation, collective, upon payment and in the interest of the same agent".

The mandate with representation allows the automatic transferability of legal effects, for the principals, of all acts that the agent performs within the limits of the mandate. The agent/principal relationship also involves joint responsibility by the passive side, which means that, for all the obligations assumed by the agent in its own business with special power of attorney, the representative power. The coordinator will be the only member of the consortium to have relations with the financial institution: it will transmit and receive statements and its own contractual statements and the ones of the various partners, it will present reports and accounts to the Commission, it will have information functions both in respect of the Commission and its partners, it will collect the money from the Commission and it will pass them quickly to the other contractors. It is the mandate binding nature which tighten the coordinator role and the fulfilment of obligations. These obligations are well defined not only in the ***consortium agreement*** (with main effects on relationships with partners) but also in the agreement with the Commission (with reference, in particular, to its relations with the latter).

The greater the care with which the parties will form the acts abovementioned, the lower the discretion held by the figure of the coordinator. In any case, both the Belgian civil law and the one of your country provide for accountability in the hands of the agent.

The coordinator will not take, with regard to partners, the hierarchical supremacy but a kind of peer over-ordering. In other words, any decision should be taken by all contractors, unanimously. An exception, however, is the power given to the coordinator to take urgent decisions which can not be postponed and which have to be then ratified (even tacitly, attributing significance to silence which assumes - so - independent legal significance) from all other *network* components. This is the rule applicable in the absence of specific provisions in the body of the *consortium agreement* in which, in the event and *ex adverso*, the parties can - as part of their regulatory autonomy - give wide (also hierarchical) powers to the coordinator, the veto power, more weight in the decision or the role of president of a real body that operates on the basis of the majority principle.

The contract of mandate will be inserted into the body of the *consortium agreement* and the choice of the coordinator is conditional upon the approval of the Commission which can decide to not accept the appointment (this happens when, for example, the organizational structure set up by the coordinator does not appear sufficient to ensure proper financial and administrative management of the project: in such cases, the Commission, in previous Framework Programmes, has come to advise the splitting of scientific and administrative coordination).

Once the role of coordinator has been assigned to one of the partners, it can be later revoked by the Commission itself (for breach of appreciable obligations) or by the partners themselves. In the latter case, however, the revocation will be possible only for just cause (dangerous breach) given the nature of mandate given, also in the interest of the agent. There may also occur the possibility of a revocation of a part of the principals by the agent. In this case, the consortium will have to follow a specific procedure indicated by the EC. You must send an official letter, with which you inform the Commission (or the relevant National Agency) about the reasons that led to decide this change, and which states that no partner has any objections in that regard. It is essential to include in this letter a description of the skills and experience of the new coordinator and its contact details. Revocation will be submitted to the attention of the European Commission itself that may, possibly, also terminate the contract, once it finds the irreconcilable conflict between the contractors and the impossibility of a successful continuation of the contractual relationship between the parties. The coordinator will also, in theory, voluntarily withdraw from the contract but, if there is not just cause, it may be required to pay damages for the benefit of the principals.

It is necessary to implement a strong organizational dedicated structure also by tracking the market for that professionalism that you do not have within your organization.

Below is attached a management model - Integrated Projects.

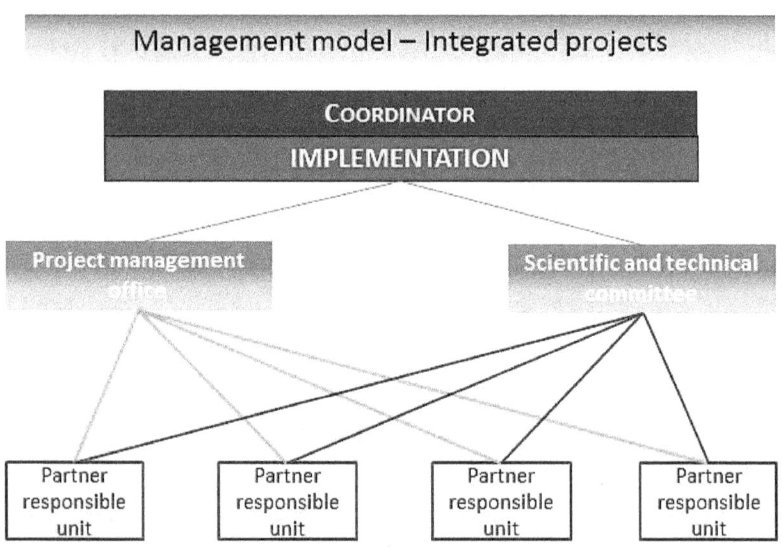

Fig. 7: Management Model (author's picture)

Integrated projects necessarily require broad participation of different stakeholders.

Each initiative planned in the project should mobilize a significant mass of physical resources, human and financial. In addition to the activities aimed specifically at the production of the tangible results of the project, there must necessarily also be a variety of activities, such as technological development, market analysis and socio-economic studies, testing, demonstration, dissemination of innovation, infrastructure and methodologies of action upgrading, management practices renewal and so on. In this context, the role and commitment of the coordinator becomes highly critical.

One of the main and most important items of expenditure will be just the one related to the partnership management. The coordinator will have to ensure the technical and organizational cohesion among members of all levels, to provide the consortium agreement and monitor its implementation, to manage contractual, financial and procedural issues, linked to the award of European funds.

In the suggested model - keep in mind that the quality and level of expertise of the management structure of the project take critical importance for success, during the selection of the proposals and the request for financial support - the coordinator will chair a board (I have called it "the Management Committee of the project") with the task of taking all the "strategic" decisions related to activities under the project proposal approved.

Probably the most delicate among the activities of the coordinator is reporting. It must send - periodically - to the European Commission a report on the activities carried out.

The report must contain:

- Summary of the activities carried out by all partners;
- Description of achievements in strict adherence to the aims pursued;
- Presentation of the progress with respect to key issues outlined in the work plan;
- Description of the problems found and corrective measures adopted;
- Illustration of complementary actions carried out by the partnership;

- Declaration, certified by an independent auditor, when expressly required by the call.

Because of the relevance, the importance, the complexity and the sensitivity of the activities that the coordinator has to play in the interests of the whole consortium, it should be highly qualified and prepared to lead the team to the full, effective and efficient implementation of the project objectives, planning and coordinating the administrative and operational activities, ensuring that allocated resources are used appropriately. It will process and evaluate ex ante ongoing methodology regarding the implementation of the project and its position will also require a high level of objectivity and independence of judgment.

Being a coordinator of a consortium has of course positive and negative sides. The first can be attributed to the role that, if done correctly, leads the organization to interface with various types of stakeholders, expanding the pool of contacts and opportunities they bring, to the greater visibility with the European Commission and the agency that runs the funding program. The latter relate to the daily and continuous project management, of which it will have all the responsibilities in financial terms. You must also always remember that you are responsible in front of the European Commission or the agency that administers the program, for all the project partners. Therefore it is good to protect yourselves in case of coordination through specific articles and clauses in the Partnership Agreement.

Useful tips:

- Always try to define with extreme accuracy, the contract between the partners, which are the rights and obligations of the coordinator, in order to reduce the degree of discretion in performing the tasks and exercising its rights.
- Adjust in the related contracts, both between partners and between partners and subcontractors, as many aspects as conceivable to limit the autonomy of action of each partner and well outline the roles, rights, responsibilities and obligations of each subject.
- Provide for the occurrence of future risks, related to the nature of the project and imagine the possible actions to limit or mitigate it. In this way you will avoid future conflicts between the partners (or between partners and subcontractors) and you will have a clear vision from the start of the actions to be taken for troubleshooting. At the same time each partner will be well aware of its role and tasks to be performed to overcome the impasse that might arise following the occurrence of certain events. Try adjusting all these aspects in contracts, perhaps by attaching a *risk management plan*.
- Always check the technical, financial and management capacity of each partner participating in a consortium, in order to have from the beginning a partnership that represents *the best of the best* in terms of

quality. This will maximize the likelihood that the project is successfully completed from the point of view of both the timing and the quality of the results and products that it will generate.

13. Roles within a European project

13.1 The project manager

The Project manager has a leading role in a project concerning its management and implementation and the lack or inexperience of that figure could fail the project execution, although the coordinator has the biggest responsibility. The Project manager has to monitor the whole project from the very first steps (partner search, planning, etc.) to the very final successful implementation. They are the decision makers who are trusted by the project, in this way they have full authority. They manage the resources (human, financial, and infrastructure) of the project and all members of the project team should support their work. Nevertheless, it is recommended to separate technical/operating management tasks and financial management tasks. Good practice says that the financial manager is a specialized figure distinct from the operations manager. Obviously, in the case of smaller projects or small organizations the roles can be mixed and a single person may hold these two functions.

13.2 Administrative staff

The administrative staff is often responsible for the correct filling of the official administrative forms during the proposal writing. Members of the staff create the list of requested documents, keep in touch with administrative staff of the other project partners and check the received forms and annexes. Consequently, the role of the administrative staff is always very important during the preparation of a proposal. Once a project proposal has been approved, the administrative staff's task is to collect all the supporting documents from the very beginning of the project implementation in order to justify the incurred costs since the Commission can require proofs to verify the eligibility of the requested payments. Usually, the administrative staff consists of 1-2 persons per project partner.

13.3 Technical experts/implementers

Technical experts provide technical information to the designer during the preparation of the project proposal. They are those who thanks to their technical skills can detail all technical aspects useful to better describe how and when provided activities may be implemented. In case of project approval, thanks to their professionalism, they assure the realization of the various tasks assigned to the partner.

13.4 Communication experts

Not all project teams have the opportunity to employ a person for communication tasks; however, there are always mandatory communication activities in each project. In these cases, for small scale projects, this kind of activities can be carried out *in-house* with the support of one or more members of the partner. In bigger and more complex projects it is strongly advised to involve a communication expert in the project team whose general tasks are the following:

- elaboration of the different communication materials (e.g., information brochures, flyers, e-newsletters);

- writing of the press releases and articles;
- taking care of media relations;
- organising press conferences and project meetings;
- checking the subcontractors (if applicable).

14. Management and monitoring

The content of the project is the key part, but the form is just as much important for the well-being of the project and the partnership, so that the content can find its best expression.
The rigor and the concreteness in the management of a project, are, in the eyes of the European Commission, at least as important as creativity and innovation that produced the project idea!
Poor project management can indeed scupper even the best ideas, resulting in partners' disaffection, loss of credibility, expenditure of energy in terms of time and commitment of the staff, targets not met and, in the worst cases, cuts of the project budget.
The project management is exemplified through 4 main areas: management, implementation, dissemination and exploitation. Often these macro areas correspond to *Work Packages*, in which are included individual activities. For immediacy of communication, we will use in the following text the term *work package* to identify these main areas, referring also to those calls that do not use them explicitly (learn more: see box below).
The most important of these macro-areas is the project implementation: below we analyse the macro-area in detail and we also give an overview of the macro-areas of dissemination and exploitation.
Some sections have been already seen in Chapter 8, since the planning of activities at the end of the development of a project

proposal and what you do instead during implementation of an approved project are closely related and consistent in the project cycle.

14.1 Implementation

Once the project is approved, it is important to implement and maintain an orderly and efficient project management, respectful of the roles and the timing provided for its successful implementation. With terms varying according to the funding program within which you move, the projects have a duration and a complexity such that the management requirements of precision and consistency, in terms of allocation of tasks, collection and presentation of documents, data, information, reporting and monitoring, become indispensable. Nothing - therefore - can be left to the individual and to the spontaneous good will of someone.

To learn more:

The work packages (WP) collect the activities of the same type, distinguishing four main macro-areas: management, implementation, dissemination and exploitation. Many calls structure their own forms distinguishing these macro-areas in which you describe in detail the activities of the same type (for example all the necessary documents to the management will be collected in the "management" work-package).

Some calls did not make use of this distinction: while performing the same tasks, they are not systematically collected in distinct work-packages.

An example is the Erasmus Plus call, dedicated to education, training, youth and sport: even if you

> perform the same activities (management, implementation, dissemination and exploitation), these are not collected within the form with the distinction in *work packages*.

Since this is such a vast subject, it is not easy to single out all the steps and you can not consider every stage of management as an element in its own right: every aspect is linked to the other and a good organizational capacity requires the ability to be able to lead the project on several parallel tracks, with the constant awareness of the interrelationship between different activities.

Logically and chronologically, the implementation of the the European project officially begins once the proposal is approved and the contract signed. At this point, the project coordinator starts using the resources defining participant teams, which will implement the activities and produce results; so, it begins to monitor the progress of the project, to manage the internal and external communication, to prepare progress and financial reports, to manage any changes and risks, and to face possible challenges and problems. In summary, the implementation phase consists of three main sub-phases with specific activities (EuropeAid Cooperation Office 2004):

→ Step 1: Starting period, planning timelines, responsibilities and activities according to the application form

→ Step 2: Implementation, through which the project leaders, on an ongoing basis, should:

a) involve people, making sure they perform tasks and provide results and that you have the necessary equipment to carry out the activities;
b) monitor and review the progress in relation to the scheduled timing;
c) re-plan the project and the activities, where necessary;

d) write progress reports.

→ Step 3: Conclusion

Despite the difficulties you can encounter, you can specify the main aspects to be organized.

Scheduling of the project timing

This activity, which does not end with the project scheduling, but rather accompanies it during the entire life cycle, consists mainly of:

- ✓ Determining the timing of work-packages (or macro-activities) development that summarize the individual activities and, more specifically, the various tasks;
- ✓ Providing on the project duration timeline, the pivotal moments in which the results will be available;
- ✓ Identifying the key steps of the project (the so-called *milestones*), and indicating the time position.

A tool widely used in project management, because it can give a vision at the same time precise and general of the project evolution and the scheduled time for the various activities, is the Gantt chart, which will be discussed later in the section 14.4, specifically dedicated to monitor the project. This will graphically show dates for the beginning and end of each activity and also show slips of non-critical tasks.

Here is a graphic example:

TASKS ALLOCATION	WP LEADER	Responsible Partner	year 1			year 2		
			G	F	Mx	G	F	Mx
			1	2	3	1	2	3
Work-Package 1: Project Management	**P1**							
T1.1: Daily management and coordination		P4						
T1.2: Kick-off meeting organisation in xxxx		P3		X				
T1.3: Information package development		P2-P4						
T1.4: Evaluation system creation		P4-P6						
T1.5: Translations		All						
T1.6: Delivery of documents for interim and final reports to the EC		P3				X		
Work-Package 2: Development of the analysis development	**P5**							
T2.1: Definition of analysis procedures		P1						
T2.2: Definition of analysis methodology		P2						

Legend: X = milestones

Allocation of tasks to project partners:

The key word is responsibility: motivating partners to be active in the promotion and implementation of the activities is the first step so that they deliver results.

In compliance with the application, the work-packages, in which are collected the individual activities, have a leader which performs alone or, more often, involving partners, the activities of which it is responsible. It is therefore very important that partners become promoters but also that they are guided by the *project manager* with a clear assignment of responsibilities, for which they are then called to account personally.

The project manager must then:

- Assign and give a more precise description of the possible roles to each party, which must have a clear vision of how to perform tasks (possibly making reference to application forms and other documents produced in the project writing phase);
- Identify the relationships among the partners' expertise and assigned tasks and possible interdependencies;
- Identify the "leader" for each activity and *work package*, in which the different activities are included. These leaders will be responsible for the good performance and the quality of the expected results for each activity and each work package.

This step involves much more than simply telling everyone what to do. With the division of tasks, is defined, in fact, the responsibility for achieving the goals. It is therefore a way to establish the individual responsibilities of each member of the team, both in relation to the project *manager* and to the other members.

The diagram on page 198 shows a possible layout and content.

Identification and measurement of available non-financial resources

It is necessary to estimate what resources are available in terms of:

- Human resources devoted to a project (number of people, skills, qualifications/certification)
- Equipment, physical instruments, space availability (quantity, type, location, ...)
- Contribution from third parties or sponsors (collaborations, subcontractors, ...)

Creating an effective coordination and management network

Establishing a coordination structure is important for several reasons: the partners must be able to share opinions, documents, contributions, in an immediate, easy and constant way; everyone must be aligned properly on the information relevant for each partner ("cascade" information are ineffective, better to choose what to say and to whom); the project is "alive", changes, improves and transforms through constant interaction and continuous updating.

The coordinator (the project manager) is responsible for general management, which is identified in the following tasks:

- Identify who does what in daily tasks (in line with what has been identified in the proposal) and their responsibilities/duties/delegation;
- Start and maintain operating procedures, or in any event provide for their delegation in time (preparation of the agenda, organization of project meetings, meeting

coordination, reporting, coordination and monitoring of activities);

- Determine, in case of more complex organisms, which is the decision-making procedure to be respected (unanimity, majority, veto options)

Dissemination and Exploitation: What are they? How to prepare a strategy

Implementation is the real heart of the project development. Next to this macro-area come up beside the dissemination and exploitation areas (following step by step the design development). The European Union, understandably, puts much interest that the funded project can reach the largest audience possible and that the benefits arising from it are widely known and exploited. The financing is a basis so that the project activities can then continue beyond the conclusion of the loan, thus giving a value to the investment that the EC has made, funding our proposal. The project results and acquired experience should therefore have the widest possible spread and a project that aims to be funded must be able to ensure that this happens.

The project results can have different forms and nature. They can consist of:

- PRODUCTS (artefacts, supports for services/information development, manuals, conferences, prototypes);
- METHODS (exchange of ideas and best practices, development of expertise on a given subject, acceleration of management skills);
- EXPERIENCE (acquired in a learning process, territorial mobility, creation of networks).

These are considered the *direct project* products. The *indirect products* are GUIDELINES of EU POLICIES (*policy lessons* derived from the development of innovative projects of particular impact or feedback on the programs undertaken) and EUROPEAN CO-OPERATION (reinforced by partnerships, intercultural dialogue, exchanges of experiences that occur in the project development).

What might be called in one word the *exploitation* of project results, actually consists of two distinct activities, although closely related to each other: the first is the dissemination and the second is a continuation of the project life after the end of the funding period (in terms of exploitation of its benefits and expansion of its impact).

We start from the theoretical definitions:

The ***dissemination*** is defined as a process designed to provide information to the target audience and key stakeholders on the quality, relevance and effectiveness of the project results and related initiatives. The dissemination becomes possible when the project results are beginning to be available, but the activities of communication and promotion have usually begun in the first months, in order to inform the public and stakeholders of the upcoming results.

The term ***exploitation*** means the activities undertaken to use and derive maximum benefit from the project results. This concept is closely related to two others: ***mainstreaming*** (transmission on channels and key interlocutors) and ***multiplication***, (obtaining a multiplier effect). In particular, through the first you circulate results obtained from the project and related initiatives on a circuit of opinion leaders and relevant stakeholders at local, regional, national, European or global level. The "multiplication", however, consists of putting in place a process by which you convince the end users of the project results to adopt/implement the outcome of projects or initiatives.

Dissemination and Exploitation: How to plan them?

Having from the beginning *dissemination* and *exploitation* plans is fundamental in European project design. For this reason it is mandatory to provide macro-activities that develop both aspects. In planning these activities, it is important to first ask yourself questions such as:
To what needs does my project provide an answer? What are the expected results? What is the target audience/industry that mainly benefit from the project results? Compared to my target/sector, in which language will I have to disseminate the results of my project?
Key elements of the *dissemination* and *exploitation* plans are:

- Types of activities planned for each of the two main activities - description, methods, mechanisms, languages used for various products/results;
- Type and amount of resources used - staff, budget, numerical quantity of the products and/or of the target to be engaged;
- Timing of activities and allocation of roles / responsibilities to partners
- The identification of a *dissemination* and *exploitation* leader to better coordinate the activities of individual partners.

Once *dissemination* and *exploitation* plans have been organized, it must be considered that they can and should be subject to continuous review and adjustment in the light of developments the project undergoes. Any change must be reported in the *Progress* and *Final Reports*.

A useful support to further deepen these aspects is the page on the website of DG Education and Culture of the European Commission:
http://ec.europa.eu/dgs/education_culture/valorisation/index_en.htm.
It is important to observe a **constant collection and documentation of all activities of dissemination and exploitation carried out**. In order to conduct this stage in a structured way, you can use a form that helps you keep track of the activities (with dedicated tools, such as wikis). A tool of this type helps to have a vision of the entire project life and not to miss any of the activities, making it available to partners for their modification and addition, and also contemplating activities not explicitly provided for in the plans for dissemination or exploitation.

14.2 Working tools

The project implementation process requires constant evaluation to determine if the actual project results are in line with the set objectives, whether they satisfy the defined quality standards and if the group is going in the right direction.
To successfully implement a European project, the manager must employ a set of methods that optimize the collection and systematization of information, supporting not only analysis, but also the decision-making process. The following instruments, some of which already presented in this guide, are very useful for the European project management:

1. Logical Framework Matrix (cf. Chapter 8);
2. Operational Plan (cf. chapter 8);
3. The progress reports (cf. paragraphs 8.3 and 14.4);
4. Risk management Matrix (cf. paragraph 14.3);

5. Gantt chart (cf. p. 85)
6. Activity diagram (cf. p. 88)

The ability of coordination, collaboration and management of project managers is fundamental to the smooth running and the proper management of European projects, as the project results are strongly influenced by both the initial design and the constant monitoring and evaluation of activities undertaken and tangible results.
Fortunately, contemporary managers now have at their disposal a variety of free and / or for fee online tools, making use of *cloud computing* and software services, to optimize the complex process of coordination of the European project.
For practical help, here are some tools mostly free, among the dozens of existing possibilities, which can help to the daily management of the projects and which facilitate the sharing among the partners, in addition to classic - and effective ! – working tools such as email, telephone and to-do-list (an actual list of activities to be performed weekly or daily).

Integrated solutions

The solutions listed below are just a sample of the type of commonly used products.

- Google +, one of the most popular and comprehensive project management platforms that includes a broad range of online collaboration, content management, communication tools and so on. Some of these tools are: Google Hangouts, used for online meetings with international partners, photos and videos sharing, screen sharing; Gmail: Google's email address; Google Docs platform for document sharing; Google Calendar, calendar that synchronizes with other Google tools,

Google Drive, a document sharing solution that offers 15GB of free storage space www.google.com

- Microsoft Office 365 - Microsoft offers a set of tools used for Project Management activities. At the time, it offers software for both Desktop and Browser, namely Microsoft Office 365 platform. A disadvantage compared to Google is that it is upon payment. www.office.microsoft.com
- Zoho Project - Applications that provide solutions for business processes, information and resource management, as well as sharing and storage services. The toolkit contains various collaboration modules (chat, meetings, wiki, etc.), related to Business (campaigns, contacts, CRM, etc.) and Productivity (work sheets, calendars, notebooks, etc.). A key component of this platform is the compatibility with Microsoft Office, which allows the simultaneous review of the documents www.zoho.com
- Wiggio - web platform that allows you to create "working groups" that share files and messages and are connected to their mailboxes. It also allows you to create to-do-list (list of tasks to be performed) with alerts on direct mail www.wiggio.com

Other working tools

- Dropbox - web platform that allows file sharing and working files that are synchronized automatically with each change made by one of the "participants" www.dropbox.com
- Skype - allows for free calls between people or groups, including chat and file transfers. www.skype.com/it
- Doodle - Google tool that facilitates the organization of meetings/conference calls. Participants can indicate

their availability, visible to all participants, avoiding mediation by mail and related waste of time. www.doodle.com

- Asana - web platform useful to organize work and create lists of tasks, assigning tasks and tracking the results www.asana.com/
- Survey Monkey - perhaps the most popular solution for online surveys, which not only creates, manages and distributes the surveys but also combines the individual results and presents them in a wide variety of sizes, suitable for almost every analysis need www.surveymonkey.com
- GoToMeeting - web conference service upon payment; it requires installation on the PC of a software by all participants. It allows you to share the screen, showing to participants pictures, presentations or websites, to make software demonstrations and to control your own computers www.gotomeeting.it
- Adobe connect Meetings - software application for upon payment, based on Adobe Flash that allows for online meetings, serves as a support to the Conference sessions, e-learning and collaborative content creation www.adobe.com/products/adobeconnect

Timesheet and timing monitoring tools

The Timesheet and timing monitoring tools provide services for time management, especially creating timesheet, sheets and other accounting documents of time and resources management.

In summary

The European project designer needs a set of online tools to manage his tasks. Here is a summary (not exhaustive) of the available tools.

File sharing	Dropbox, Google Drive, Wiggio, Microsoft Storage
Information sharing	Wiggio, Confluence, Media Wiki, Google Docs, Office Docs
Online documents writing	Google Docs, Office 365, Zoho Office
Task Management	Asana, Zoho Task Management, Office Project
Meeting Online	Skype, Google Hangouts, Go to meeting, Adobe connect Meetings
Task Tracking	Asana
Timesheets e timing monitoring	Are available on internet some solutions upon payment
Project scheduling	Office Project, Open Project, Gannt Diagrammer (Google Applications)

14.3 Risk and Quality

Planning how to handle potential project risks should be described already in the proposal, implemented from the beginning of the project and, if necessary, revised during implementation. The risk analysis is applied during the initial period, identifying the conditions on the basis of the logical framework matrix. In this way you will have a proper assessment of the importance of the possible cases in terms of potential (strong / low) impact and (high / low) likelihood. On the basis of this matrix, for example, if it is assumed that for a specific or general goal or task there is a risk and this is estimated to have major impact on the project implementation and high likelihood, this risk is considered a "killer assumption". This implies that it is necessary to find an alternative, otherwise the feasibility of the project itself can be compromised.

The analysis and the ongoing project risks review should be carried out in a systematic way during the project management. However, there should always be alternatives for continuing the project implementation; which does not mean that the project activities should not be taken as too risky, since a prerequisite, because of the degree of congenital uncertainty, could also lead to a scenario better than expected.

Risk Management Matrix

A matrix typically used in risk planning and management is the following one. The matrix takes the following conditions:
Probability
(1) low: the occurrence of this risk is not very likely;
(2) average: this risk may occur;
(3) high: it is very likely that this risk will occur;
Impact
(1) Low: This risk has a low impact on the results and activities of this project and has no implications for budget or planning;
(2) average: this risk has a significant impact on the results of the project and requires adjustments in results, budget and / or planning;

(3): high: this risk jeopardizes the success of the project, affecting the exploitation. It has important consequences for budgeting, planning, Consortium and results.

Risk	Likelihood (L)	Impact (I)	TOTAL (L x I)	Preventive action	Necessary adjustments
X	1	1	1	....	....
Y	3	2	6	....	....

The product between the two areas (L) and (I) gives you a scale of values, in multiples of 3, from 1 to 9. Total results from 6 onwards are placed in the "red zone" which requires careful assessment of countermeasures if the risk materializes in a negative event.

Intellectual property

The issue of intellectual property is a very sensitive aspect because many projects develop products, knowledge, prototypes of which it is then necessary to determine ownership and use. The issue is particularly acute in research and technological innovation projects, where the results exploitation in terms of intellectual property (from which could potentially arise economic exploitation of results) often becomes a central point to be defined with consortium partners from the beginning.

First, you need to give some definitions. The European Commission in research projects distinguishes between the concepts of *foreground* and *background*. The ***foreground*** is the set of results, including information, materials and knowledge, generated within a project. It includes Intellectual Property Rights, such as patents, and not protected know-how. The *foreground* is thus something both tangible (prototypes, dissemination materials, codes,..) and intangible but, however, **directly linked to the project development.**

The ***background*** is that set of information and knowledge (including inventions, databases, etc.) **owned by the project participants before the signing of the Grant Agreement** and relevant with respect to the realization of the project. The *Background* is not regulated in the Intellectual Property management of the programs financed by the European Union, although in fact it is an established practice (especially in R & D, Innovation) that already in proposal preparation involved parties sign agreements of intellectual property and confidentiality to protect the mutual background.

The *foreground,* or the result in terms of products and knowledge from project development, is owned by the person who generated the result. In the case of a partnership, it is held in a shared way, unless the partners agree otherwise. The partners must reach an agreement on the allocation of intellectual property rights through an agreement called *IPR Agreement - Intellectual Property Rights Agreement.*

The IPR is a strategic document and especially a legally valid contract between the parties, aimed at establishing the rights to the use of project results. In the case of programs of culture and education in general it must be submitted after the project has reached the end of the eligibility period. In research projects, however, as you can easily understand, it takes a greater value, becoming, in fact, a preliminary document to the contract and in many cases the call includes as eligibility requirement to attach it to the proposal. It is normally prepared by the project coordinator, but this is not a necessary requirement. In addition, there is a default format. In general, though, it is good that the document will address the following points:

- Involved parties: list of partners included in the project;

- Subject: objectives of the agreement (e.g. prescribe the use of a given project result);
- Material: a fundamental part of the document as it identifies the exact cause of the element in which to establish property rights (e.g. Manual of the project after the end of the loan agreement, new products, new production process etc.). The material can include any type of element: from electronic documents, to training courses, databases, etc. If it comes to transnational projects, many of the products will be translated into several languages so each product in each language is considered as a separate element.
- Duties in the use of the material: where possible, you should always refer to the fact that the product has been made possible thanks to other partners, but above all must be mentioned the financial support of the European Union (with their own logo and disclaimer). Each of the partners must ensure that the material will be subject to dissemination. However, this will only take place after the existence of an IPR agreement.
- Use by a third party: the transfer to third parties of the project results (or *foreground*, in the case of research projects) should happen with the rights passage of both people and organizations. There are no special rules, except the need that among the project partners there is agreement and following notification.

A related use of third-party, consists of commercialisation, which is also subject of discussion and formal agreement.

Since this is a binding agreement, each project partner must have an original copy of the IPR agreement.

There is a site of the European Commission, responsible to solve doubts and to get updates on the topic: http://www.iprhelpdesk.eu/

How to deal with issues of confidentiality and information security (Confidentiality and Data safety)

It is strongly recommended that the obligations concerning the confidentiality of information are always detailed in the Consortium Agreement. Any information that you want to share only with a small group of people, must be explicitly indicated as confidential in each step of the project. Each party, including the European Commission, must take measures to ensure that this aspect is guaranteed, even after the end of the project. The Grant Agreement contains two articles that refer respectively to the confidentiality of the data and their security.

Confidentiality

The beneficiaries and the Commission commit to undertake any measure that is aimed at preserving the character of confidentiality of information, documents or products recognized as confidential in relation to the execution of the project.
This obligation will terminate when:

- The confidential information becomes publicly available in a manner that does not violate the covenant of confidentiality
- The confidential information is transmitted to a third party that has no obligation to respect confidentiality and has therefore the right to make it public

- The publication of confidential information is provided for or made possible by other measures in the Grant Agreement

Data protection

The Grant Agreement also addresses the issue of sensitive data protection.
It states that all information contained in the document must be managed in accordance with the provisions of Regulation (EC) No 45/2001 of the European Parliament and the Council on the proper use of personal data by the institutions and bodies of the Union European.
(Http://eur-lex.europa.eu/LexUriServ/LexUriServ.do?uri=OJ:L:2001:008:0001:0022:it:PDF).
Such information may only be used strictly for implementation and monitoring / evaluation activities of what is provided in the loan agreement (including the possibility of transferring such information to entities that have been identified for the sole purpose of monitoring or verifying these activities).
The beneficiaries of the loan, upon written request, can have access to their personal data and correct information that is incorrect or incomplete. They can also send a note at any time to the European Ombudsman for Data Protection if they consider there has been an improper use of their personal data.

Deviations and changes

The project is alive! The necessary rigor in managing a project does not mean rigidity.
Effective management of a project results in a balanced mix of rigor and organizational flexibility, being able to adapt itself to conditions and instances that were not foreseen or budgeted at the time of writing the application form.
Notwithstanding the fact that the project was selected among all its competitors because of what was "promised" in the application form, changes, not too impactful, are still allowed and their management is free for coordinator and partners. Considered the "evolutionary" feature of a project, it is assumed that all programming will be subject to review or major deviations or rather adaptations during implementation. However, the risk is that they take over, if not properly channelled. To limit this risk, it is important to stick to activities of constant control and verification of adherence to the timing, providing:

1. frequent project meetings (one per month - remotely and one every four to five months - face to face);
2. rather frequent reports of technical and financial progress;
3. extraordinary meeting to correct any deviations or urgent issues.

Especially for point 2, I mean in addition to the two internal reports mandatory under the grant agreement (interim and final reports). For example, the interim report is presented in mid-project and it could be a year or more after the start, if only here you realize certain issues, it may already be too late to correct them. If, however, you organize a quarterly monitoring system, the same problems emerge much earlier with relating corrective actions that you will have plenty of time to put in place.

Following, some of the most significant changes and how to manage them.

How to change the budget over the life of the project

Changing the structure of the project budget is planned and permitted in certain cases through Amendments to the budget itself and consequently to the *grant agreement.* The communication has to be sent to the National Agency (in the case of decentralized projects) or the European Commission, through **formal written request for modification, only when the movement of money between two eligible budget headings** (for example from staff to operational - travel, machinery, sub-suppliers etc. - costs), **determines an increase on item increased greater than a maximum percentage established**, regardless of the type of an adjustment between the various operating costs. This is a general rule valid for all Programs, within each of which you may identify different situations. The suggestion, then, is always to refer to the guides for the *applicant* for each program. The change request must be submitted through a dedicated space in the Request for Change form (*Amendment Form*), attaching the required documents.
To facilitate understanding, it provides a practical example with reference to a program in which the minimum shift of budget, without resorting to a formal request for changes, corresponds to 10%:

- If you need to move 3,000 Euros from "staff" to "operating" costs items amounting to 70,000 euro, you do not need to send any formal request for changes to the Agency, as 3,000 euro represents less than 10% of 70,000 euro. Otherwise, if it was moving 8,000 euro towards the item that already includes 70,000 Euros, you should send a formal request for changes of the budget composition.

- If you intend to increase the budget dedicated to staff costs from EUR 15,000 to 18,000 you will have to make a written request in that it is a change of more than 10%, even if on the same budget item. Consequently, you will have to turn down other items of the budget to allow this increase. Do not forget, in fact, that the total approved should remain unchanged.

In the evaluation of the final report, the National Agency or the European Commission will stick to this same rule, putting attention to the fact that the changes made to the individual items do not affect the result and the quality of results.

As for indirect costs, you can not make similar changes, since their funding is already limited to a certain percentage of direct costs.

In any case, you can modify the total budget, the amount or percentage of financing recognized.

You must make sure, also, that the **change request is received at least 4/6 months before the end of the eligibility period (less is very likely that the request will be rejected)** and that the costs presented in the reporting have been approved **before** they are incurred. **The retroactive costs** incurred (not provided in the Grant Agreement and not yet approved by Amendment) **are not considered eligible.**

How to handle a change of partner / coordinator

In the event that the consortium had to make a change to its composition (for replacement or exit from one of the project partners), must **send written notification** to the National Agency or the European Commission (depending on the program), through the form of formal amendment (*Amendment Form*), attaching the required documents.
In case the change affects the project coordinator, that is the party signing the financing agreement, the replacing partner will be liable with regard to the presentation of all the documents, certifying the costs already incurred and will receive from the outgoing coordinator an updated and accurate account of the activities already implemented and the expenditure incurred, before it withdraws permanently from the project.
Also in this case you need to send a formal request for changes to the Agency by a special section of the Amendment Form. This, once approved in the changes, will be signed by both the outgoing and replacing coordinators.
A formal request for modification must be submitted even if the coordinator should remain the same but with a different name or address (or company name).
The suggestion is always to read carefully the "guide for applicant" of each program that you are going to use and above all, to think well to all aspects in the process of writing the project proposal, so as to reduce the changes just only if they are necessary.

Other changes for which you need to submit an *amendment form* and wait for the acceptance of the request in order the change to produce effect:

- Change to the eligibility period;

- Change to the budget;
- Change to the bank account;
- Change to the *work programme*.

For any other changes that you should need and for which you are not sure whether or not to submit a formal request, do not be discouraged, write to your project officer and ask for enlightenment!

14.4 Project monitoring

Project Monitoring System

An important phase of any project is the monitoring, carried out by the beneficiary and the managing authority, which is the institution which manages and administers the funding program. Monitoring is a regular activity, which includes systematically collecting, sorting, aggregation and storage of information: it is necessary for a project assessment and control.

The monitoring of the project is based on information, coming from data provided by the beneficiary, materials regarding the implementation, as well as data provided by the information system.

This information is used to assess whether the progress of the project adheres to its schedule and timing provided, both for content and financial aspects. In case of delay, the monitoring system serves to highlight areas of operation and suitable corrective measures. Monitoring should take place at both project and program level. The information gathered from the projects then populates the databases useful for the Commission in monitoring the entire program. The outputs of the monitoring are called monitoring reports.

To learn more

- **What is a monitoring report**?

It is a comprehensive report by the beneficiary on the progress of project activities and other obligations under the contract.

- Objective

Giving an indication of the project progress, using measurable indicators, about possible deviations with content and expenses planned;

- Content and form

It is standardized and binding for all parties involved in the monitoring and evaluation process.

- When?

In periods planned by the Managing Authority and through electronic submission, in writing, together with the required attachments. Not submitting monitoring reports is considered as a breach of contract. The beneficiary is responsible for the accuracy, correctness, veracity and completeness of the information provided.

- Type

a) mid term monitoring report submitted by the recipient during the implementation of project activities, for example, every six months;

b) final monitoring report - presented by the beneficiary at a deadline set by the Managing Authority from the end of the project activities;

c) report on the project participants - (only for some programs): the beneficiary presents separate information on participants in the project during the implementation of activities;

d) Follow-up monitoring report - submitted by the

beneficiaries after the end of the project - within 5 to 3 years.

- Attachments (examples)

a) the minutes of project meetings;
b) time sheets;
c) photographic documentation of the training activities carried out;
d) copies of newspaper articles;
e) TV or radio spot relating to the project.

- Importance

A lot! The monitoring reports, in fact, collect project information, valuable for the evaluation, on the basis of which the Managing Authority has the right to carry out spot checks, to suspend payments, seek a refund, cancel the contract, etc.

Audit and monitoring visits

It is not uncommon during the period of project implementation but also after the end that the funding authority organizes audits on the project.

Checks can concern:

1. formal correctness (correctness of administrative documents generated and compliance with the fundamental principles of public procurement, namely: equal treatment, non-discrimination of bidders, transparency, efficiency and effectiveness);
2. substantial correctness (evaluation of the objective activities implementation);
3. financial accuracy (evaluation of eligibility of expenditure, history expenses, compliance with the methods of payment).

In real life, these areas are not as rigidly separate. A verification during the project implementation will examine one or more of these aspects. Instead, a check after the end of the project usually will focus primarily on the first and third field.

The checks can be made at the headquarters of each project partner, although, as a matter of major efficiency, in reality the coordinator undergoes them. At other times, especially the coordinator, might be invited to the headquarters of the funding authority for verification. In one or the other case, the check is always announced and organized with the subject; the EC or its delegated agencies anticipate in any case in writing the checklist of the areas that will be audited.

Interim reports

Is the project is on the right track? This is the key question for the entire project monitoring process. This represents the important information that consortium, stakeholders, potential donors, and most importantly, the project manager, need to know.

Monitoring can be understood as a more-or-less continuous process of reviewing the progress of activities, compared to the initial plan and considering the implementation of various aspects, such as:

a) the completion of activities;
b) the deadlines and times;
c) the availability of (human, material and financial) resources;
d) the extent to which the desired effects have been achieved;

e) the level of budget spending;
f) the extent to which the objectives and the results have been achieved;
g) changes that occurred during the project development, which directly affect the activities

The monitoring process must be studied in the planning stages of the project, on the basis of the logical framework matrix, which includes measures of four levels of analysis: overall objective, specific objective, activities and results, as shown above. In this sense, the formulation of clear objectives is essential to facilitate the process of monitoring the project results: it is useful to define the objectives using the "SMART" technique. The objectives must be:

- **S**pecific to the objective that should be measured;
- **M**easurable (qualitatively or quantitatively);
- **A**vailable (available at an acceptable cost);
- **R**elevant (relevant to the information needs of managers/evaluators);
- **T**ime bound (defined in time so you know when you can expect that the target is reached).

In addition, according to the formulation of objectives in the logical framework matrix there must be defined objectively verifiable indicators, which give a clear and unambiguous measure of achievement of these objectives.

The monitoring phases may be identified broadly as follows:

Step 1 - Collection of documentation and information (facts, remarks and assessments), which should take into account:

a) Indicators relevant to the objectives set out in the logical framework matrix;
b) Quality and relevance of the activities and resources used;
c) Project impact;
d) Relationships with the target groups and partners.

Phase 2 - Analysis and preparation of the results, determined by:

a) Comparison between expected and achieved results, including unexpected outcomes, deviations identification and analysis;
b) Comparison between planned and implemented procedures, as regards the project organization and the relationship with the target groups.

Step 3 - Formulation of recommendations and proposed corrective action, in order to allow possible adjustments, such as for example: timing, resources, goals, and design procedures in use.

Monitoring Tools

In preparing the steps abovementioned, there are different models used to track the project progress, which allow a better overview and analysis of the information and conclusions such as:

a) GANTT chart: it can be a great tool, as well as for planning and implementation (described above), also for monitoring, allowing a better view of the project progress, while providing a complete analytical reading of what it was planned and what has been realized for a certain period of time in terms of tasks, calendars, defined resources, budget, etc..

ACTIVITY	CALENDAR (Months)					HR	MR	COSTS	RO	RS	OA
Activity 1 planned											
A1 performed											
Activity 2 planned											
A2 *performed*											

HR: Human Resources
MR: Material Resources
RO: Responsible Organisation
RS: Responsible Staff
OA: Objectives Achieved

b) **Descriptive report table**, built on the basis of the structure of the logical framework matrix (EuropeAid Cooperation Office 2004):

Ref. No	**RESULTS, DESCRIPTION AND INDICATORS**	**EXPECTED TARGETS/ RESULTS IN THE REPORTING PERIOD**	**PROGRESS / PROBLEMS**	**ACTION REQUIRED**

The report preparation

Usually, funding agencies provide guidelines for the preparation of reports, giving instructions regarding the content and format to follow, specific models, the deadlines for submission of the reports, etc. This is a first element to be considered for the drawing up of reports, to avoid duplication, procedures and parallel documents. The report is intended to inform on the project progress and to see if what was promised, agreed and contracted in the project proposal was subsequently implemented. In this way the funding authority will check in a structured way and according to standard procedures if the funds were spent appropriately.

Although the reporting is considered a costly task, in terms of time and resources, it is of fundamental importance. There is often a major investment in obtaining information, which goes hand in hand with a lack of systematization, organization and analysis of information gathered. Moreover, even in cases where the information is analysed, often it does not occur in good time to adequately drive the decision-making processes.

The added value of any relationship lies precisely in its utility, as a support, systematization and organization tool, through which significant amounts of information can be interpreted and transformed into useful knowledge for interventions of continuous improvement.

Which reports should be produced? How often?

The answer to this question depends on the nature and duration of the project; however, reports can be of the following types:

1. An initial report: elaborated three months after the start of the project, focusing on issues of particular importance, e.g. substantial changes between what was planned and what will be achieved.
2. Progress status: processed on a semester basis.
3. Annual report: it applies to long-term projects and should include the project progress, accompanied by a brief description of the annual reviews of the project, reflecting improvements and corrective actions.
4. Final report: it is prepared at the end of the funding period of the project and contains all the information needed for an integrated vision of the project, including recommendations, lessons learned and possible follow-up actions. To know what are the most important issues

that should be addressed by the report, you must answer the following questions (Ulrich Schiefer, 2006):

a) Who should read this report? What features should it have? What information should it provide?
b) What kind of document is it? What are the features of this document?
c) What is the purpose of the document and what is its utility?
d) When and how often should the report be elaborated?

While preparing the reports, you must keep in mind, especially in terms of writing techniques and language used, the various actors who could read it: in particular those who have direct interest in "reading" the report, such as: target groups, stakeholders, team and *project managers*, (national and international) sponsoring organizations, funding authorities, national and international authorities.

Objectively Verifiable Indicators (OVI)

Objectively verifiable indicators are an essential tool to monitor and assess the status of implementation in relation to the program objectives. These are used to evaluate possible savings (minimizing the costs necessary to carry out the activities or the goods, works and services provision, while maintaining the appropriate level and quality), efficiency (maximizing the activity results in relation to available public funds) and effectiveness (relationship between expected and actual results, considering the investment of public money) of the funds allocated to the project.

Objectively verifiable indicators are:

A. program indicators,
B. project indicators, namely: result indicators and impact indicators

Indicators can be defined according to their measurability:
The quantitative indicators concerning the number of results, activities, products (e.g., the number of trainees, the number of publications produced, the rate of participation in a conference).
Qualitative indicators are not strictly measurable though they may be objectively verifiable (e.g. the acquisition of skills, changes in behaviour or habits, etc.)

Useful tips:
For a correct management system, do not forget to:

- Establish an effective communication system;
- Provide clear partnership agreements, stipulating in writing all the rights and responsibilities of each partner;
- Use the kick-off meeting to clarify the arrangements for implementing the project, the work plans and the internal communication strategy;
- Distribute evenly and with care tasks between partners, according to their skills and abilities; make sure there is no duplication of work;
- Ensure that all partners have access to the necessary project documents;
- Make sure the tasks are clearly and accurately explained and that everyone understands its role in the project;
- Establish a clear system of labour division and

effective monitoring to guide partners;

- Remember the deadlines in time;
- Apply a clear and simple style of communication, avoiding too complex sentences;
- Try to involve partners as much as possible with a regular request for feedback, opinions and suggestions;
- Remember that one of the main reasons why partnerships fail and do not lead to positive results is the lack of clear and timely communication;
- Ensure transparency to the partners, in particular with regard to administrative and financial matters.

How to manage your project team:

- Empower the project team on the activities and reports to be drawn up;
- Design a good management plan, providing benchmarks to evaluate the performance, results quality and efficiency;
- Maintain a constant quality control, comparing expected results and achievements; where necessary, taking prompt corrective measures;
- Consider the type of information you need and avoid an overload of irrelevant information;
- Provide templates for documents; specify the structure, character and templates (models) of the requested documents, in due time;
- Ensure that tangible results collected by the team are consistent with each other;
- Avoid accumulating work at the last moment, which usually leads to a lower quality of the results;

- Strictly follow the guidelines and rules laid down by the European Commission, especially concerning the dissemination and sustainability of project results.

Report: how to write?

- Adapt the report to the expected reader;
- Produce briefing and useful papers, that meet the reader's interests and needs;
- Provide information, targeted to the action, as support to the decision-making process;
- Provide objective, transparent and comprehensive information: the use of clear and friendly language improves the understanding of the report;
- Use summaries, elements that facilitate quick location of information (indices), elements that provide a better view of documents (graphs, tables, images, etc.).
- Organize and systematize the content, allowing the reader to easily find the information requested;
- Find the proper size for the document. A good practice to compile a report of adequate size is the rule of the disaggregation levels: the abstract should contain information which is strictly essential, the summary contains key information, the body of the report should be brief and concise, and all detailed information should be aggregated within appendices, attachments or ancillary documents.

Some helpful tips for *project management*

- Carefully plan each task and check regularly if the progress phases are met;
- Regularly monitor project costs and get help from an expert, involving him in decisions before engaging in expenditures; later it may be too late!
- Check that the other partners have the situation under control;
- Write an 'internal" global report at least every 6 months and at least four months before the end of the project, so that you can inform the Commission of any significant changes and be able to ask an amendment in time, if necessary;
- Review regularly the contract and the eligibility rules;
- Keep on a regular basis during the life of the project any document supporting activities and related costs;
- Study in time the necessary forms;
- Contact your project officer in case of doubt.

SECTION 4 BUDGET PREPARATION AND MANAGEMENT

15 Preparing the budget

In this section we will focus only on the process of creating the budget, deferring instead to the dedicated section regarding accountability. This section will help the reader not to "get lost" and to better outline the two aspects even aware, however, that in actual operations, the two areas are increasingly closely linked. In fact, the correct methodological process is always to build the budget during the writing of the proposal already thinking about when those values need to be accounted for. It is a specular process: preparing a budget following the financial rules of the program and while preparing it already thinking about when and how you will report back those costs in case of approval is the best way to start creating a sustainable budget.

The drafting of the budget and therefore its management, if and when the proposal is approved, depends mainly on whether the budget meets the financial rules of the budget built and operated in "real costs" or the budgets built and operated according to the "lump-sum" rules.

In the first case the budget in real costs, as the expression already indicates, are those in which each cost inserted refers to real or market quotes, or to the reality of the organization involved in the project. In this way there are many variables that can make rise up or down values for *partners*, even more when residing in different countries, but even in the same country. Think about the typical differences there may be between the salaries perhaps for equal function, or differences in the costs of travel and accommodation, the contracting of goods or services suppliers and so on in dozens if not hundreds of different examples.

So, the budget in real costs, to be created with knowledge of the facts, requires input, that a good coordinator must require from each partner, especially those related to personnel costs. The latter, in fact, is the call that absorbs most of the entire budget, but it is also the one that more than others in reporting phase must be treated and monitored with extreme care.
The consequence of this system is that in the reporting process will be considered eligible only the costs that can be verified by invoices, receipts, payroll, contracts, transfers and so on. In other words through a mass of documents, the purpose of which is to prove that the given cost is just a "real cost", in the sense of contingent in relation to the place and the subject that has sustained the costs.
In the early stages of verification of expenditure, in the budget in real costs, the funding authority, in addition to judging the quality of the results, will focus on how the budget has been used and then it will check completely or partially all the supporting documents relating to one or more expenses.
In a budget in pure "lump-sum" or "unit" costs, however, the input values are predetermined and fixed whatever the subjective circumstances of the partners or the country of origin. These values can be related to personnel costs, travel expenses and other types of costs. In this case when the program provides this mode, it will also provide all the parameters (typically tables) to easily calculate the budget of the proposal (see par. 9.1 for more details).
Therefore, when a budget is built, managed and accounted for in this way, at least in the reporting process it is not required to produce any documentary evidence in order to demonstrate how the eligible costs have been spent. The funding authority will focus its controls especially on the verification of the quality and sustainability of the results. The fact remains, however, that beneficiaries must still produce and store all

documentation relating to the expenditure, because if within five years from the final payment the project is subjected to Audit, these documents should be made available and verified. A description of the documents to be presented in reporting when working with this kind of budget will be presented in Chapter 17.2.

15.1 The common rules

Eligible costs

To be considered as eligible, costs must satisfy the following general criteria:

- They must relate to activities involving the **countries** that are eligible to participate in the programme. Any costs relating to activities undertaken outside these countries or by organizations not registered in an eligible country are not eligible unless they are necessary for the completion of the project and duly justified in the application form. Any amendment to the activities that involves other countries must have the prior specific approval of the Commission or executive agency. Certain costs incurred in third countries participating or in their regard are eligible;
- They must be incurred by the **legal persons / organizations official partners of the consortium**; costs incurred by individuals are not eligible.
- They must be **connected** with the action (i.e. directly related to the execution of the project in accordance with the work plan);
- They must be **necessary** for performance of the project;
- They must be **reasonable and justified** and they must accord with the principles of **sound financial**

management, in particular in terms of value for money and cost-effectiveness;

- They must be **generated** during the lifetime of the action, i.e. during the eligibility period between the dates of beginning and end of the project. This window of time is always written in the *grant agreement*;
- They must be **actually incurred** by the beneficiary and members of the consortium, be recorded in their accounting books in accordance with the applicable accounting principles and be declared in accordance with the requirements of the applicable tax and social legislation in the Country of the Partner;
- They must be **identifiable and verifiable**.

Value added tax

The VAT is considered an eligible cost **only if** it is not recoverable under the existing national legislation on VAT (typical cases are associations or non-profit organizations, in general). The only exception is for those activities or transactions in which federal, state and local authorities and other public bodies are involved as public authorities.

Non-eligible costs

The following costs can not be held in any way eligible:

- return on capital;
- debts and debt service charges;
- provisions for losses or potential future liabilities (provisions for contractual and moral obligations, fines, financial penalties and legal costs);
- interest owed;
- doubtful debts;

- exchange losses;
- VAT (see above paragraph on value added tax);
- costs declared by the applicant and covered by another action or work programme receiving a European Union grant or any other source of funding;
- excessive or reckless expenditure;
- purchase of capital assets;
- in case of rental or leasing of equipment, the cost of any buy-out option at the end of the lease or rental period;
- costs associated with the preparation of the application;
- costs of opening and operating bank accounts (costs of transferring funds are eligible);
- other costs incurred to any document required to be submitted with the application (e.g. audit reports, etc.).

Eligible direct costs

The eligible direct costs for the action are those costs which, with due regard for the conditions of eligibility set out above, are identifiable as specific costs directly linked to performance of the action and which can therefore be booked to it directly. The categories of eligible direct costs are specified in the following pages and can be divided in the following types:

1. staff costs
2. travel and subsistence costs
3. costs of equipment or materials
4. costs of subcontracting
5. other direct costs

A particular category is represented by indirect costs or otherwise called Overheads.

Indirect costs

Indirect costs are those costs which, with due regard for the conditions of eligibility, are neither identifiable as specific costs directly linked to performance of the action nor can be booked to it directly, but which have nevertheless been incurred during the management of the project. The indirect costs of the project eligible for European funding are a fixed lump-sum depending on the program equal to a certain percentage of the total amount of eligible direct costs. (**WARNING: always check the *work programme* and the reference call. A notable exception is represented by the fact that ERASMUS Plus does not provide for reimbursement of indirect costs**). Such costs need not be justified by accounting documents.

Indirect costs shall not be eligible under a project grant awarded to a beneficiary which is already receiving an operating grant from the Commission during the period in question. Examples of indirect costs are:

- all costs for equipment related to the administration of the project (i.e. as computers, mobile phones etc.).
- communication costs (postage, fax, telephone, mailing, etc.).
- infrastructure costs (rent, electricity, etc.) of the premises where the project is being carried out;
- office supplies;
- photocopies.

15.2 Construction of a budget in real costs: the main items of an EU project

What follows is proposed to provide the technical elements in order to draw up a proper and sustainable budget in accordance with the EU financial rules, that is prepared in line

with the real values existing in the country and in the reality of the partner organization. The fact remains, however, that only constant study and experience will be able to provide that little extra something that can make you untangle without fear in the myriad of specific cases that may arise.
The following guidelines must always be looked at a mirror image with respect to the stage where a certain budget, that we are building here, will then have to be reported. In fact, if at the beginning the rules should be applied to create the budget and then **focus on the eligibility rules of expenditure**, they should then be applied with **focus on the verification of expenditure** and that is how they were realized.

A. Direct costs:

A.1. Staff costs:

Staff costs refer to the costs for the staff involved in the project. The European Commission or its Delegates Agencies distinguishes four main categories of staff: Manager, Researcher / Lecturer, Technical and Administrative. Staff costs are calculated on the basis of working days defined in the project proposal. The models for all types of report are provided by the Commission. An **example** of how to calculate staff costs is presented below.

First, the project proposal defines the days assigned to each Work Package or macro-area:

WP NO	WP TITLE	Task	WORKING DAYS FOR STAFF				
			M	R	T	A	TOT
WP1	**Management**	……	20	-	-	20	40
WPx	**Dissemination**	….	-	40	15	5	60

M: Manager
R: Researcher
T: Technical staff
A: Administrative staff

Second, the table of the budget of the project proposal provides the daily cost of staff, usually in Excel format. This cost shall be identified according to two alternatives:

1. Based on the maximum ceilings for each country of the program, if required by the call itself.
2. According to the pure real cost existing in the partner organization.

In case 1, it means that, subject to the requirement for partners to allocate the real cost per day for its staff, the maximum limit for the calculation of the contribution (e.g. 70% or 80%) is determined by a ceiling announced by the Commission for that role in that particular country. In other words, if a partner were to have the daily costs of its staff above the ceiling, it must first ascribe the real value, knowing that, for the calculation of the contribution, the funding authority will stop at the ceiling in place. This applies in all cases that, for any budget item, refer to the ceilings.

Case 2 instead occurs when ascribing the daily cost of staff or other items of expenditure, you must refer to any ceiling. We ascribe what is the real cost for that item of expenditure.

Using the example of the previous table, insert the daily cost of the various professional figures.

MANAGER			RESEARCHER			TECHNICAL			ADMINISTRATIVE		
W	D	T	W	D	T	W	D	T	W	D	T
20	150	3.000	40	100	4.000	15	80	1.200	25	60	1.500

W: working days
D: daily cost
T: total

For a subject to be considered "staff", whose cost can become accountable in related category, it must fall into one of the two following cases:

1. Statutory staff, having either a permanent or a temporary individual contract with a partner of the consortium. To be considered in this category, staff must report to the relevant partner organisation as an employee;
2. Temporary staff recruited through a specialised external agency by any of the consortium partners.

The concept of "dependence" of point 1, refers to the current practice that admits to a subject, not framed in the partner organization chart with a contract of dependence (whatever administrative form it takes), to be treated as staff assimilated to employees and as such, accounted in the "Staff" budget if his contract meets these conditions (a typical example are "in house consultant" or "self employed" collaborators)

1. duration of the contract at least equal to the lifetime of the project;
2. involvement of the subject in activities implemented throughout the duration of the project

3. preparation of monthly *time sheet* addressed to the subject, with a summary of the time spent on the project and the activities carried out.

Costs related to staff working in subcontracting or clear contracts with external consultants, shall be included under the category "*Subcontracting costs*" (see below). Staff members of Project partners are not allowed to operate in a subcontracting capacity for the project.

For all the partners' staff:

1. The rate of the country in which the partner organisation is registered will be applied, independent of where the tasks will be executed (i.e. a staff member of an organisation of Country A working fully or partly in Country B will be budgeted on the basis of the rates of Country A).
2. Real daily staff cost rates are based on average rates corresponding to the applicant's usual policy on remuneration, comprising actual salaries plus social security charges and other statutory costs included in the remuneration. Non- statutory costs such as bonuses, leased car, expense account schemes, incentive payments or profit-sharing schemes are excluded.

A.2. Operating costs:

- ***Travel and Subsistence***: European projects generally include transnational activities, as the kick-off meeting and management meetings, training courses, seminars, conferences and many more. Therefore, the project members need to travel.

Travel costs are allocated on the basis of actual cost.

1. Travel costs for staff taking part in the project are allowable, provided that they are in line with each partner's usual practices on travel costs
2. Costs may be claimed only for journeys directly connected to **specific** and clearly **identifiable** project-related activities. For information on charging Travel Costs for non staff members please refer to Section "Other Costs" and "Subcontracting Costs".
3. The travel cost for a journey should include all costs and all means for travel from the point of origin to the point of destination (and vice versa) and may include visa fees, travel insurance and cancellation costs.
4. Reimbursement is based on real costs, independent of the means of travel chosen (rail, bus, taxi, plane, hire car). Partners are required to use the cheapest means of travel (e.g. use best value for money tickets for air travel and take advantage of reduced fares, where this is not the case then a full explanation should be provided).
5. Expenses for private car travel (personal or company cars), where substantiated and where the price is not excessive, will be refunded as follows (whichever is the cheapest):
    - either a rate per km in accordance with the internal rules of the organisation concerned up to a max of €0.22;
    - or the price of a rail, bus or plane ticket (see point (3) above). Only one ticket shall be reimbursed, independently of the number of people travelling in the same vehicle.
6. For hire cars (maximum category B or equivalent) or taxis: the actual cost where this is not excessive compared with other means of travel (also taking account of any influencing factors such as time, large volume of

luggage due to the nature of the project). Reimbursement takes place independently of the number of people travelling in the same vehicle.

Moreover subsistence costs of staff travelling to another participating country in the context of project development are also eligible. The budget should have as a reference the maximum rate ***eventually*** set out in the single call or in the financial rules of the program. Any surplus will be considered ineligible. The applicable rate is that of the country of destination, i.e. the country in which the living expenses are incurred.

1. Costs may be claimed only for journeys directly connected to specific and clearly identifiable project-related activities.
2. Reimbursement is based on the existing internal rules of the Partner organisations, which may be on an actual cost (reimbursement of receipts) or daily allowance basis. In either case, proof of attendance and overnight accommodation will be required to substantiate declared costs at reporting stage.
3. Subsistence rates cover accommodation, meals and all local travel costs at the place of destination abroad (but not local travel costs incurred to travel from place of origin to place of destination). In calculating the number of days for which to apply the Daily Subsistence Rate it should be noted that a FULL day normally includes an overnight stay.

Eligible subsistence costs are calculated on the basis of scales of eligible unit costs, as explicitly listed in the call of reference. Otherwise, the listing of these costs will be made on the basis of justifiable actual costs. The resulting amounts will be included in the budget and will be taken into account when calculating the European Union contribution.

- ***Subcontracting***: The term refers to the involvement of third parties (not part of the consortium) for the implementation of some project activities. Subcontracting is necessary when the consortium does not have the required capabilities. The coordinator or the partners of the consortium sign a contract with a subcontractor for the supply of goods and / or services, according to which is poured the sum identified in the budget. A typical example of subcontracting for EU projects is to sign a contract with an external evaluator of the project. Subcontracting for web design, website hosting, logo and another virtual identity is just as common.

In order to preserve the essence of the project partnership, management and general administration of the project may not be subcontracted.
Costs are calculated on the basis of a verifiable estimate or, if the subcontractor is already identified in accordance with the procedures set out in paragraphs from 1 to 4 below, on the basis of an offer. The estimate / offer will cover all costs (staff costs, travel costs, etc.).
The beneficiary will award the contract to the bid offering the best value for money or, respectively, to the bid quoting the lowest price, in accordance with the principles of transparency and equal treatment of potential contractors and taking care to avoid conflicts of interest.
Pay attention to compliance with specific conditions for the award of a contract to a subcontractor, depending on what is required by the call or regulations on transparency in

government procurement. In this regard you may find in the call a paragraph whose content is like the following: (WARNING - IT IS PURELY AN EXAMPLE)

1. payments of amounts not exceeding € 12,500 in respect of items of expenditure may consist simply in payment against invoices, without prior acceptance of a tender;
2. contracts with a value between € 12,500 and up to € 25,000 are subject to a procedure involving at least three tenderers, following a call for tenders;
3. contracts with a value between € 25,000 and up to € 60,000, are subject to a procedure involving at least five tenderers, following a call for tenders;
4. for contracts with a value over € 60,000, national rules with regard to procurement apply.

The total cost of subcontracts can not exceed, as a rule, 30 per cent of the total direct costs of the project. Lower percentages may be provided with differences from program to program. (**WARNING: always check the *work programme* and the call of reference**).

- ***Equipment***: Some projects require the purchase of some equipment and / or consumer goods, to implement specific project activities. For example, if a project includes training activities, the partner may need to obtain training materials, such as a PC, a video projector, a multimedia board, etc. Similarly in a Research & Development project you might need machinery or equipment to carry out or realize project activities. In this case you may undertake their purchase or rental. But WARNING!! In case of **purchase**, it is not the cost of the property tax that you can put in the budget, but a portion calculated in proportion to the percentage use in the project, just for the period of use of the property within the project, applied on the annual value of depreciation of the asset. An example will illustrate the concept.

P	Description	Justification	Total cost	Mode	Annual depreciation	Period of use in the project (months)	% of use in the project	Eligible cost
1	equipment X	....	5.000,00	Purchase	25%	9	50%	468,75

- In case, however, of rental / lease, the project partners no longer having the ownership of the property, on the same assumptions above, the eligible cost changes. In this case, you should not take into account in your calculations the values related to depreciation.

P	Description	Justification	Mode	Total cost (sum of the rental invoices on-year)	Period of use in the project (months)	% of use in the project	Eligible cost
1	equipment X	....	leasing	5.000,00	9	50%	1.875,00

- Please note that the program should **explicitly** define the purchase of equipment such as eligible costs, otherwise they will not be reimbursed.

- ***Other expenses (if provided by the program)***: costs not covered in any of the budget lines, above, are considered other costs. Other costs are allocated on the basis of actual costs incurred, as well as for everything else, do not forget that you are moving in the area of budget in "real costs"! The category "Other costs" can only contain costs incurred by the partners themselves.

These are costs arising directly from:

- requirements imposed by the Grant Agreement are eligible (dissemination of information, specific evaluation of the action, audits, reproduction, translation etc.), including the costs of any financial services (notably the cost of financial guarantees);
- the realisation of specific activities or of products/results of the project are eligible (e.g. the organisation of seminars where the seminar is foreseen as a product/result and where task-related costs are easily identifiable), the production of proceedings of a seminar, the production of a video, the purchase of product-related consumables (reams of paper for printing of publications, blank DVD), etc.
- When travel and/or subsistence costs are reimbursed to third parties (i.e. for the costs of people who are neither staff of the partners in the consortium, nor subcontractors), the rules applicable to the reimbursement of costs for staff of the partners in the consortium will be applied.

In certain cases, other costs which are not covered by the other cost categories mentioned above may also be considered eligible. Some examples are: one-off costs for press releases and publicity, purchase of copyrights and other Intellectual Property Rights, purchase of information materials (books, studies and electronic data); conference fees; registration fees for conferences; rental of exhibition space, etc.

All costs related to the administration of the project (consumables, ancillary materials, photocopying costs,

telephone costs, paper, etc.), are covered by indirect costs of the project.
Also for "other costs", where set under the Programme, you must comply with the rules for the awarding of positions already analysed in the previous chapter concerning "*subcontracts*"

16 "Unit cost" Lump-sum Budget

When the financial rules of a program involve such circumstances, as described in paragraph 15.2, budgets are constructed by referring to the tables that contain the input values for each item in the budget. A series of very schematic tables will clarify the concept better than a thousand words!
The following examples refer to ERASMUS +, but conceptually apply to any program which follows this approach. In fact, ERASMUS + and other programs that use this approach provide extensive documentation to be able to easily follow the rules in order to calculate the values to be included in the budget.

16.1 The typical budget headings of the plans with "unit cost" lump-sum budget

1. Project management and implementation
2. Transnational project meetings
3. Products / Intellectuals Outputs
4. Broadcasting events
5. Exceptional costs
6. Special needs support (specific entry for ERASMUS +)
7. Learning, teaching and training activities - Travel and individual support (specific entry for ERASMUS +)

8. Learning, teaching and training activities - Individual support and language support (specific entry for ERASMUS +)

Project management and implementation

Eligible costs	• Management of the project activities (costs for planning, coordination and communication between the project partners); • Development of materials, tools, approaches for small-scale learning, teaching and training; • Virtual cooperation and for local project activities (e.g. Learning projects in class, work activities for young people, teaching or training organisation); • Information, promotion and dissemination activities (e.g. brochures, flyers, websites, etc.).
Amounts of funding	It is a recognized unit monthly contribution per participating organization based on the duration of the Partnership and the number of partners: • € 500,00 for the coordinator • € 250,00 for the partner Maximum € 2.750,00 per month.

Transnational project meetings

Eligible costs	Costs incurred for participation in the partnership meeting governing the organization and implementation of project activities, hosted by one of the partners, among participants in the initiative.
Amounts of funding	It is recognized a contribution to the costs of travel and subsistance on the basis of unit costs slots: • For distances between 100 km and 1999 km € 575 per participant and per meeting • For distances over 2000 km financing is € 760 per participant and per meeting. Up to 100 km is not expected contribution. Travel distances will be calculated using the distance calculator provided by the European Commission: http://ec.europa.eu/programmes/erasmus-plus/tools/distance_en.htm The **annual ceiling** per project amounts to € 23,000

Creative works/Products/Intellectual outputs

Eligible costs	Costs related to the achievement of results and intellectual products of the project (e.g.: curricula, teaching materials, OER - open educational resources, IT tools, analysis, peer-learning methods).
Amounts of funding	Contribution for the costs of staff involved on the basis of unit costs. For the calculation of staff costs it is necessary to refer to the specific tables in the programme guide, which provides the daily rates per country, for the 4 eligible professional categories: • **Manager**; • **Teacher, trainer, researcher, youth worker;** • **Technical staff;** • **Administrative staff.** http://ec.europa.eu/programmes/erasmus-plus/documents/erasmus-plus-programme-guide_en.pdf. The amount due depends on the profile of the staff and the country of the partner. Costs related to **managers** and **administrative staff involved in the management and implementation of the project must be considered in the budget heading "Project management and implementation"**. To avoid any overlap of these costs, the applicant must justify the nature and volume of the expenditure indicated for the staff referring to each result/intellectual product expected. The **output** expected should be **substantial** in quality and quantity.

Maximum daily rates per Country for the 4 eligible professional figures

Source: http://ec.europa.eu/programmes/erasmus-plus/documents/erasmus-plus-programme-guide_en.pdf

Countries	Manager	Teacher/Trainer/Researcher/Youth worker	Technician	Administrative staff
Denmark, Ireland, Luxembourg, Netherlands, Austria, Sweden, Liechtenstein, Norway	294	241	190	157
Belgium, Germany, France, Italy, Finland, United Kingdom, Iceland	280	214	162	131
Czech Republic, Greece, Spain, Cyprus, Malta, Portugal, Slovenia	164	137	102	78
Bulgaria, Estonia, Croatia, Latvia, Lithuania, Hungary, Poland, Romania, Slovakia, former Yugoslav Republic of Macedonia, Turkey	88	74	55	39

Dissemination events

Eligible costs	• **Expenses related to the organization** of conferences, seminars, events aimed at the diffusion and dissemination, at national and transnational level, of intellectual product **resulting from the project**; • **The costs of travel and accommodation of the members of the project partner organizations involved in the event are excluded from this budget heading.**
Amounts of funding	Contribution on the basis of unit costs: • For local participants (persons belonging to the country where the event is held) is planned an amount of € 100 per participant; • For transnational participants (individuals from countries other than those in which the event is held) is planned an amount of € 200

	per participant. The maximum amount is € 30,000 **per project**. The financial support is recognized only to the **dissemination events directly related to the dissemination of results / intellectual products resulting** from the project. Therefore, a project that does not involve the creation of intellectual achievements can not receive funding for dissemination.

Exceptional costs

Eligible costs	• Costs related to subcontracting or to the purchase of goods and services; • **Costs related to a financial guarantee, if required**. **The budget heading is based on** the recognition of a percentage of the actual eligible costs incurred.
Amounts of funding	• The European contribution will be equal to **75% of the total eligible costs**, up to a maximum of € 50,000 per project (excluding costs for the bank guarantee). • In case of purchase of assets only the depreciation is eligible. Subcontracting is recognized eligible only for those services that can not be provided directly by the partner organizations in the initiative, and duly justified. The purchase of equipment shall not affect the normal office equipment or those normally used by the organizations participating in the project.

Special needs support

Eligible costs	• Additional expenses **directly related to participants with disabilities. They include costs directly related to participants with special needs and their companions who take part in mobility activities;** **This may include costs related to travel and subsistence if justified and if not already requested a contribution for such participants in the budget category "travel and individual support".**
Amounts of funding	• The budget heading is based on the **recognition of the actual eligible costs incurred.** For all costs incurred, the European contribution will be **100% of the total eligible costs.** • The request for such costs must be duly justified in the application form.

Learning, teaching and training activities – Travel and individual support

Eligible costs	Travel: it is recognized a **contribution based on unit costs to travel costs of participants, including accompanying persons, from the place of origin to the point of carrying out the activity and return**. For distances between 100km and 1999Km 275 €/per participant. For distances of 2000km and over: €360/per participant; Individual support: a daily cost is **recognized on the basis of unit costs relating to the subsistence cost of the participants, including accompanying persons, during the activities**. The costs must be calculated according to the type of mobility (short or long term) and at the duration, referring to the specification table of the Guide of the Erasmus +: http://ec.europa.eu/programmes/erasmus-plus/documents /erasmus-plus-programme-guide_en.pdf (see p. 118). The promoter must show that the mobility activities are necessary to achieve the objectives and results of the project.
Amounts of funding	The travel distances will be calculated using the **distance calculator** provided by the EC: http://ec.europa.eu/programmes/erasmus-plus/tools/distance_en.htm.

Learning, teaching and training activities - Language support

Eligible costs	**Eligible costs of transnational mobility are linked to the support provided to participants in order to improve knowledge of the language of instruction or work.** **The request for financial support must be mentioned in the application form and applies to languages not offered by the online centre service.**
Amounts of funding	They are unit costs only for activities that have a duration between 2 and 12 months: 150 € per participant requiring language support.

16.2 EU funds and project co-financing

Almost all EU funds require co-financing by the project consortium. This means that each partner in the project consortium has the obligation to co-finance its activities. In general, approximately between 20% and 30% of the total budget must be covered by the partners. For example, if the project budget is € 100,000, the total contribution of the partners is equal to € 20,000 - € 30,000, which will be distributed among the partners in proportion to the percentage of their involvement. Take note of the fact that the share capital, to ensure the initiative, almost never can be covered by in-kind assets (see the program) and almost never requires the payment in cash of the share. What normally happens is that the part is covered by the workloads/man assured by partners, through the personnel involved in the

project, who receive a salary of 100 that will be invoiced as such, although the share "reimbursed" by the project will be for example, of 60, 70 or 80. By the same mechanism, a sub-contractor paid 100 and accounted for that value, will see a "refund" charged to the project of 60, 70 or 80 and so on. The difference is precisely the contribution of partners to co-finance the project.
I said almost all, because some programs or certain actions of some programs provide a contribution of 100%, so have no co-financing by the beneficiaries. For example, the Horizon 2020 program for research activities carried out by universities and/or public entities provides for a contribution of 100%. The ERASMUS Plus also, for numerous actions, (e.g. Strategic Partnerships) provides for a contribution of 100% (so there is no co-financing) except for the heading "Exceptional costs" where the contribution is 75%. **The latter is a clear example of mixed funding mechanisms.**

17 The financing and administrative reporting

Correct procedures and constant financial and administrative monitoring, are the basis of a generally excellent management of a European project. Unfortunately there are still many who believe that the success of a project depends primarily on how the project has been implemented from a technical standpoint, then the quality of the results and/or products obtained. It is not uncommon to see, instead, focus on the issues of budget and financial monitoring. The consequence of all this is to see excellent projects from the point of view of results ending badly their contractual life, suffering from cuts and budget reductions operated during the final verification of the costs and in the worst cases, through procedures for revocation or recovery funds, due in good faith to oversights, misinterpretation of financial rules or more simply, by not taking the necessary time to properly manage the finances of the project. Proper financial management of a project, relies above all on skills needed in people who deal with this area.

Some of the essential skills that a financial manager must have are:

- Specific and in-depth knowledge of European financial rules, which govern the program in question.
- Accounting: As the whole reporting task is about the numbers, the financial manager should have basic accounting skills.
- Documentation: The financial manager must keep and file properly all the expenses' documents, including payrolls, timesheets, invoices, sub-contracts etc., as these are essential for both reporting purposes and also for smooth financial management. The authority generally asks partners to keep the documents up to 5 years after the end date of the project.
- Time management: Each project is implemented within a particular time frame. Therefore, financial managers must be able to adhere to strict deadlines and prioritize tasks.
- Communication & Team Work: Team working and good communication skills are also very important as financial managers need to provide guidelines and lead the partners while preparing their individual financial reporting. A strong, dynamic and functional communication network among partners makes the financial management and reporting much easier.
- Stress Management: Dealing with money might be stressful as financial reporting errors could create

undesired and tense situations. Thus, financial managers should get used to working under pressure.

- Budget and Cash Management: What to pay? When to pay? How much to pay? How to manage objectives if in case of payment delays? These are crucial questions for a financial manager to keep in mind at each project phase.

17.1 Reporting on real costs: Summary of documentation per budget heading

The reporting of a project based on a "real costs" budget feeds itself on the same rules used in preparing the budget. I invite you to refer to those described in chapter 9.2. If during the preparation of the proposal these rules were to be considered primarily in terms of eligibility of costs (then decide if a cost could be eligible and if so, any conditions of eligibility), when reporting such rules are to be considered above all, with respect to the accountability of that particular cost. Let us recall that in reporting it is assumed that such costs have already been incurred, documented and paid. To reduce or eliminate the risk that certain expenses, although considered eligible at the beginning, are no longer eligible at the end (e.g. for errors related to the time of payment, or related to the dates of the invoice or receipt, or for failure to comply with the ceilings, where they exist, for the breach of the procurement procedures and so on), the financial manager should from day one of the project set up an internal monitoring system for its and other partners organisations so that the occurrence of such problems is immediately noticed and solutions, wherever possible, can be implemented.

We propose below a summary table, by budget heading, that illustrates the minimum documentation required during the reporting and the most common mistakes to avoid.

BUDGET HEADING	SUPPORTING DOCUMENTS	COMMON MISTAKES
STAFF ACCOUNTING	• contracts, *timesheet* and list of activities undertaken, invoices/payroll, bank payment, contribution payments in the workplace; • calculation method used to identify the daily gross cost of the person; • unpaid voluntary collaboration is not permissible.	• failure to comply with the ceilings allowed (if any); • lack of supporting documents; • error in calculating the unit cost; • confusion among staff and subcontract.
TRAVEL AND SUBSISTENCE	• tickets and invoices + boarding pass, proof of payment; • justification for travel; • invoices and receipts for all costs declared.	• failure to comply with the ceilings allowed (if any); • lack of supporting documents; • error in calculating the number of days to be considered.

BUDGET HEADING	SUPPORTING DOCUMENTS	COMMON MISTAKES
EQUIPMENT	• invoices, proof of payment; • supporting documents in case of *"procurement procedure"*.	• lack of supporting documents and above all, in case of "procurement procedure"; • miscalculation of amounts attributable.
SUBCONTRACTING	• initial offer very detailed; • contract that identifies activities to be performed, the timing, the operating period, the amount and the terms of payment; • detailed invoices (activity actually performed and number of hours worked, cost), proof of payment; • supporting documents in case of "*procurement procedure*".	• lack of supporting documents and especially in the case of "*procurement procedure*"; • confusion among staff and subcontractors.

BUDGET HEADING	SUPPORTING DOCUMENTS	COMMON MISTAKES
OTHER COSTS	• contracts, invoices, proof of payment; • supporting documents in case of "*procurement procedure*".	• lack of supporting documents and especially in case of "*procurement procedure*"; • indirect costs declared incorrectly in the category "other costs".

Always pay close attention if the call provides in particular for the budget headings *subcontract*, equipment and other costs, the activation of procedures of so-called "*procurement*" or contract notice. In other words, procedures that provide for the need to launch a tender to award the contract for supply or service. The tender could have a "privatistic" management (i.e. valid for private entities, not public) within a certain amount for which the contractor decides the rules for participation and the criteria for the award of any merit scores. In other cases, for example when the amount of the contract exceeds certain limits you may need to launch, instead, a process of public tender following the rules existing in the country of residence of the partners (over the limit, where specified, all public and private bodies should enable the public evidence).

Below there is an example of what you might find specified in the program:

- Contracts with a value up to € 12,500 may be paid upon presentation of one single invoice without competition.

- Contracts with a value between € 12,500 and € 25,000 are subject to a procedure involving at least three tenderers.
- Contracts with a a value between € 25,000 and up to € 60,000, are subject to a procedure involving at least five tenderers;
- Contracts with a value over € 60,000, are subject to the tender procedures valid in the country of the beneficiary of the project.

My advice is to always read the program carefully to be certain how to handle these issues.

17.2 Lump sum reporting: Summary of documentation per budget heading

In order to clarify the administrative reporting path of a budget managed at lump-sum costs in the "Unit Cost" model I will use here summaries that follow the same order used in chapter 16.1., when the same costs were addressed but in the framework of the budget construction. The first row of each table briefly recalls the method of calculation of the cost. Remember that all the figures are an example, and are still relative to Erasmus Plus - strategic partnerships action. The goal is still to explain the context and methodology of calculation. The figures, the ceilings may change depending on the Program, but not the bottom line.

Rules for reporting the project management and implementation costs

Calculation of the amount of contribution	N° of months of Project lifetime X unitary contribution (coordinator € 500, Partner 250 €).
Defining event	The Beneficiary must implement the activities and achieve objectives expected and covered by this category of expenditure.
Supporting documents	Description of the activities and objectives in the Final Report and the Dissemination Platform (store in any case expenses evidences and any supporting documents).

Rules for reporting the transnational project meetings costs

Calculation of the amount of contribution	Total N° of participants X applicable unit contribution (€ 575 for distances between 100 and 1999 km, € 760 for distances > 2000km).
Defining event	The Beneficiary must have taken part in the transnational project event and done the trip reported.
Supporting documents	Certificates of participation issued and signed by the host partner. Hotel bill.

Rules for reporting the costs of realization of products / intellectual outputs

Calculation of the amount of contribution	N ° of staff working days X daily unit cost (amount varies depending on the category of staff and the country in which the beneficiary is established).
Defining event	The intellectual property must have achieved a level of acceptable quality and must comply with the characteristics presented in the application stage.
Supporting documents	- Description of the Dissemination Platform; - Time Sheet; - Employment contracts or evidence for the staff belonging to the Beneficiary.

Rules for reporting the costs related to dissemination events

Calculation of the amount of contribution	N° of participants (from different organizations, from those of the beneficiary and the other project partner organizations) X applicable unit cost (€ 100 for local participant, € 200 per international participant, excluding Project Partners).
Defining event	The multiplier event must have taken place and should have an acceptable quality level.

Supporting documents	- Description in the Final Report; - Sheets with signature of the presence of the participants; - Detailed agenda; - Copy of documents used / distributed during the event.

Rules for reporting the exceptional costs

Calculation of the amount of contribution	The contribution is equal to the reimbursement of: a) 75% of eligible costs actually incurred; b) € 50,000 excluding the costs of a financial guarantee if required by the Agreement, depending on which of the two amounts is the lowest.
Defining event	- Subcontracting: the purchase of goods and services if requested by the beneficiary and approved by NA, - Financial security: costs relating to a guarantee of pre-financing submitted by the beneficiary if required by the NA; - Depreciation of equipment or other goods.
Supporting documents	- Subcontracting: invoices; - Financial guarantee: proof of the cost of the financial security; - Depreciation: proof of purchase, rental or lease of equipment (always validate the rule of depreciation per rate of use).

Rules for reporting the costs associated with special needs (CASE OF ERASMUS +)

Calculation of the amount of contribution	Refund of 100% of the eligible costs actually incurred.
Defining event	Expenditures that are necessary to enable persons with special needs to participate in the project, and which are in addition to unit costs.
Supporting documents	Invoices of actual costs incurred;

Rules for reporting the costs of the activities of learning, teaching and training - Travel and individual support (CASE OF ERASMUS +)

Calculation of the amount of contribution	Travel: N° of participants X unit contribution (depending on distance bracket). Individual support: N° of participants X length of stay (Amount varies depending on the type of activity and the country).
Defining event	Travel: the participant must have actually embarked on the journey reported. Individual support: the participant must have undertaken the activities abroad.

Supporting documents	Travel: certificate of participation issued and signed by the host organisation. Individual support: certificate of participation.

Rules for reporting the costs of the activities of learning, teaching and training - language support (CASE OF ERASMUS +)

Calculation of the amount of contribution	Language support: N° of participants X unit cost.
Defining event	Language support: the participant must have actually taken up an activity abroad longer than 2 months and performed linguistic preparation.
Supporting documents	Language support: certificate, invoices etc.

Useful tips:

- Carefully plan every activity and check regularly if the progress phases are met;
- Regularly monitor project costs and get help from an expert, involving him in decisions before realizing the costs; later it may be too late!
- Check that the other partners have the situation under control;
- Write an 'internal' global financial report at least every 6 months and at least four months before the end of the project, so you can ask for an amendment within the legal time limits, if necessary;
- Re-read regularly the contract and the eligibility rules;
- Keep on a regular basis during the lifetime of the project any supporting document of undertaken activities and related costs;
- Study on time the necessary financial forms;
- Contact your project officer in case of doubt.

Financial Kit

This supporting toolkit to the administrative and financial project management, prepared by the Commission, aims to help recipients of EU funds for external actions to comply with the financial management rules stipulated in the EU contracts. It is a toolkit providing practical guidance for financial managers, such as how to identify important risk areas, what are the tricky areas, what might go wrong and how to avoid risks that can be easily avoided. The document also presents best practices, tools and templates. Further, the toolkit is designed as an educational training program and covers 8 different modules:

- Module 1: Internal Controls
- Module 2: Documentation, Filling and Record Keeping
- Module 3: Procurement
- Module 4: Asset Management
- Module 5: Payroll and Time Management
- Module 6: Cash and Bank Management
- Module 7: Accounting
- Module 8: Financial Reporting*

These modules, as well as other useful tools and templates, can be found at:
http://eacea.ec.europa.eu/about/documents/fik_1202.pdf

It is highly recommended for financial managers to study these training modules before starting their project. However, please be aware that the Commission notes that: "The toolkit is not a set of rules in addition to the existing legal, contractual and regulatory framework".

More details and useful tips for Financial Reporting are summarised in the following chapter.

The interim and final financial reports

The internal procedures of proper financial and administrative monitoring have their two important moments in the preparation of the interim and final reports. These are the two moments required by the contract in which the coordinator, on behalf of all the other partners from which he or she acquires the relevant data, presents to the financing authority the "state of the art" of the project budget management. A good rule would be, as already mentioned, to set internal procedures for monitoring regardless of the formal moments in which to present these reports. Failure to submit the necessary reports may result in the termination of the contract and the restitution of the amounts already paid and recovered.

Relationships are really essential for the following purposes:

- Check that the funds were used in accordance with the objectives, activities and budget specified in the contract;
- Inform the contracting authority on the progress of activities (for interim reports);
- Determine the final amount of the EU contribution to the project.

What could go wrong?

Some of the problematic areas during the project reporting stage are presented below:

- The financial reports must be in accordance with the conditions defined in the contract by the Agency.

Otherwise, the Contracting authority may cancel the contract and even reclaim the amounts paid in previous payments. Thus, financial managers must ensure that financial records are kept up-to-date. They must also adhere to the reporting deadlines.

- Some supporting documents, providing an evidence for the eligibility of the expenses, might be missed out. Thus, managers should be careful to include all the supporting documents and/or accounting records (bank statements, invoices and etc.). The financial reports must be in accordance with the underlying accounting records. Also, the supporting documents must provide a proper trail from the accounting records. Giving clear reference numbers to the supporting documents and providing these in all relevant parts of the financial report is very useful as it makes the reporting much more comprehensive.
- The classification of the different budget headings may not be clearly mirrored in the financial report. This may cause confusion and rejection of the report by the Agency. The financial manager must prepare the financial report in accordance with the classification used in the budget. This is also useful in comparing the actual expenses with the envisaged budget.
- The currency rate may cause some problems for partners outside of the Euro zone. If the correct exchange rate is not used, the authority may conduct some deductions in the payments. The financial manager should consider the exchange rate identified in the contract for all expenses that need currency exchange. The official website of the Commission for the exchange rates is:

http://ec.europa.eu/budget/contracts_grants/info_contracts/inforeuro/inforeuro_en.cfm

- The financial report must cover all the funding sources used in the project.

5 golden rules to prepare good financial reports

- Drafting financial reports is a must!

"All contracts for EU funded external actions (except supply and works contracts) require the Recipient to submit financial reports to the Contracting Authority. Failure to submit these reports may cause the Contracting Authority to terminate the contract and to recover any amounts already paid and not substantiated. If the project is audited, the lack of a financial report may cause the auditors to issue a disclaimer report (declaring that it is impossible to formulate an opinion on the project's financial report). This could result in the Contracting Authority deciding to recover any funds paid."

- The financial report must be aligned with the accounting records.

"Recipients should arrange for a clear audit trail from the financial report to the accounting records and the underlying supporting documents. If there is no proper audit trail, any auditors might declare the financial report to be un-auditable. The consequences for the Recipient might be the same as if no financial report was submitted at all. Ideally, the financial report should directly tally with the accounting records, account by account, line by line, without any addition, grouping, adjustment or omission. If this is not possible, the Recipient should at least draft a clear reconciliation between the two. This reconciliation should be kept in the project documentation."

- Financial reports must mirror the classification used in the budget.

"It is essential to draft the financial report using the same classifications as in the agreed budget. This budget, annexed to the Contract, is the only budget version that matters. This requirement is vital to allow budgeted and actual expenditure to be compared."

- Financial reports must be drafted in the correct currency.

"It is essential to draft the financial report in the same currency as that used in the agreed budget, usually the euro. The currency is specified in the special conditions of the Contract. It is the currency in which the EU contribution is denominated. This requirement is vital to allow budgeted and actual expenditure to be compared. Recipients must follow the rules laid down in the Contract when converting expenditure in local currency into the reporting currency."

- Financial reports must cover all sources of project funding.

"The financial report must cover the entire project and not just that part of it financed by the EU. For grant contracts, the general conditions require that "the financial report shall cover the action as a whole, regardless of which part of it is financed by the Contracting Authority". It is essential to comply with this rule, as the EU grant is calculated as a share of the total eligible costs of the project."[11]

---

[11] All the quotes of paragraph "5 golden rules to prepare good financial reports" come from Financial Kit: http://eacea.ec.europa.eu/about/documents/fik_1202.pdf

Appendix: Main European Programmes in Direct Financing

Programme	Sector	Managed by	Objectives
LFE2014-2020	Environment	DG Environment DG Climate Action EASME	The Life program is an instrument of EU funding for environment and climate action; The general objective of LIFE is to contribute to the implementation, updating and development of European policies and legislation on the environment and climate, by financing projects with European added value. http://ec.europa.eu/environment/life/
Erasmus+	Education, Training, Youth, Sport	EACEA Erasmus+ National Agencies	The Erasmus Programme + is designed to support the efforts of the countries participating in the program aimed to use, effectively, the potential of European social and human capital. It is based on the principle of lifelong learning, by linking support to formal, non-formal and informal learning in the fields of education, training and youth. The program also strengthens the opportunities for cooperation and mobility. The program also pursues the objective of developing the European dimension in sport, by promoting cooperation between agencies responsible for the sector. Erasmus + also supports actions, cooperation and instruments consistent with the objectives of Europe 2020 and its flagship initiatives such as Youth

Programme	Sector	Managed by	Objectives
Erasmus+	Education, Training, Youth, Sport	EACEA Erasmus+ National Agencies	on the Move and the agenda for new skills and jobs. Through the open methods of coordination the program also helps to achieve the objectives set by the strategic framework for European cooperation in education and training and the European strategy for youth. In particular, the Erasmus + contributes to: • the objectives of the Europe 2020 strategy, including the main focus on education; • the objectives of the strategic framework for European cooperation in education and training ("ET2020"), including the corresponding benchmarks; • sustainable development of third countries in the field of higher education; • general objectives of the renewed framework for European cooperation in the youth field (2010-2018); • the objective of developing the European dimension of sport, especially grassroots sport, in accordance with the Union work plan for sport; • the promotion of European values in

Programme	Sector	Managed by	Objectives
Erasmus+	Education, Training, Youth, Sport	EACEA Erasmus+ National Agencies	accordance with Article 2 of the Treaty on European Union. http://eacea.ec.europa.eu/erasmus-plus_en
Justice Program 2014-2020	Justice	DG Justice	This program will contribute to the further development of a European area of justice based on mutual recognition and mutual trust. It promotes in particular: judicial cooperation in civil and criminal issues, judicial training, effective access to justice in the EU, the drug policy. http://ec.europa.eu/justice/grants1/programmes-2014-2020/justice/index_en.htm

Programme	Sector	Managed by	Objectives
Justice Program 2014-2020	Justice	DG Justice	This program will contribute to the further development of a European area of justice based on mutual recognition and mutual trust. It promotes in particular: judicial cooperation in civil and criminal issues, judicial training, effective access to justice in the EU, the drug policy. http://ec.europa.eu/justice/grants1/programmes-2014-2020/justice/index_en.htm
Rights, Equality & Citizenship Program 2014-2020	Human rights, equality, fight against violence and discrimination, data protection	DG Justice	This program will contribute to the further development of a Europe in which equality and rights of persons. Its nine specific objectives are: promote non-discrimination; combat racism, xenophobia, homophobia and other forms of intolerance; promote rights of persons with disabilities; promote equality between women and men and gender mainstreaming; prevent violence against children, young people, women and other groups at risk (Daphne); promote the rights of the child; ensure the highest level of data protection; promote the rights deriving from Union citizenship; enforce consumer rights http://ec.europa.eu/justice/grants1/programmes-2014-2020/rec/index_en.htm

Horizon 2020	Research & Innovation	DG Research & Innovation EASME ERC EIB	Framework Programme of the European Commission for research and innovation. Objectives of Horizon 2020: • Response to the economic crisis: investment in jobs and growth; • Topics related to well-being, safety and environment; • Strengthening of the position of the EU worldwide; • Networking opportunities between European companies The structure of Horizon 2020 consists of 3 priorities or pillars, which are implemented through specific programs and a specific financial aid: - Excellent Science - Industrial Leadership - Societal Challenges http://ec.europa.eu/programmes/horizon2020/ Participant Portal http://ec.europa.eu/research/participants/portal/desktop/en/home.html National Contact Point APRE http://www.apre.it/5366

EuropAid	Development and International Cooperation	DG International Cooperation & Development (EuropAid)	DG EuropeAid has the task of developing EU policies on development and providing assistance worldwide. EuropeAid delivers aid through a series of financial instruments, pledging to ensure the quality and effectiveness of EU assistance. As an active and proactive subject in the development, it promotes good governance, human and economic development and tackles universal issues, such as fighting hunger and preserving natural resources. https://ec.europa.eu/europeaid/node/1071
EaSI Employment and Social Innovation	Employment, Social Innovation, Fight against poverty	DG Employment and Social Affairs	The program for employment and social innovation (EaSI) is a European financial instrument that aims to promote a high level of high quality sustainable employment, to guarantee adequate and dignified social protection, to fight against exclusion and poverty and to improve working conditions. It consists of 3 axes that support: • modernization of social policies and work with the axis PROGRESS • professional mobility with the axis EURES • access to microfinance and social entrepreneurship with the axis microfinance and social entrepreneurship http://ec.europa.eu/social/main.jsp?langId=en&catId=1081

Programme	Sector	Managed by	Objectives
EaSI Employment and Social Innovation	Employment, Social Innovation, Fight against poverty	DG Employment and Social Affairs	The program for employment and social innovation (EaSI) is a European financial instrument that aims to promote a high level of high quality sustainable employment, to guarantee adequate and dignified social protection, to fight against exclusion and poverty and to improve working conditions. It consists of 3 axes that support: • modernization of social policies and work with the axis **PROGRESS** • professional mobility with the axis **EURES** • access to microfinance and social entrepreneurship with the axis **microfinance and social entrepreneurship** http://ec.europa.eu/social/main.jsp?langId=en&catId=1081

Programme	Sector	Managed by	Objectives
Creative Europe	Culture, Audiovisual creativity	EACEA	Creative Europe is the framework program dedicated to the cultural and creative sector for 2014-2020, made up of two sub-programs (Culture and Media) and a cross-section (the guarantee fund for the cultural and creative industries). The general objectives of the program are to promote and safeguard European linguistic and cultural diversity; strengthen the competitiveness of the cultural and creative sector to promote smart, sustainable and inclusive economic growth. Specific objectives: • to support the ability of the European cultural and creative sector to operate transnationally; • to promote the transnational circulation of cultural and creative works and cultural operators; • to strengthen the financial capacity of the cultural and creative sectors, in particular of SMEs;

Programme	Sector	Managed by	Objectives
			• to support transnational policy cooperation in order to promote innovation, policy development, audience building and new business models. http://eacea.ec.europa.eu/creative-europe_en
Europe for Citizens	Active citizenship	EACEA DG Immigration	In order to achieve reconciliation among the citizens of the European Union, the Europe for Citizens Programme shall contribute to the following general objectives: to contribute to the understanding, by the citizens, the EU's history and cultural diversity that characterizes it; to promote European citizenship and improve conditions for democratic civic participation at a European Union level. http://eacea.ec.europa.eu/europe-for-citizens_en National Contact Point (EPC) for Italy http://www.europacittadini.it/index.php?it/94/ecp-italy

Programme	Sector	Managed by	Objectives
COSME - Competitiveness of Enterprises and SME	Enterprise internal market, competition	DG for Internal Market, Industry, Entrepreneurship and SMEs EASME	**Access to financing** COSME aims to make it easier for small and medium-sized enterprises (SMEs) access to finance at all stages of their life cycle - creation, expansion or transfer of business. Thanks to the support of the European Union, companies have easier access to guarantees, loans and equity. EU financial instruments are channelled through local financial institutions in the countries of the Union. To find a financial institution in your country, visit the portal of access to finance. **Opening of the markets** COSME helps companies to gain access to EU and non-EU markets. The program supports the Enterprise Europe Network, which helps SMEs to find business and technology partners and understand EU legislation. COSME also funds the Your Europe portal, which provides practical information on how to exercise economic activity within Europe, and the portal for the internationalization of SMEs for companies wishing to develop their activities

Programme	Sector	Managed by	Objectives
COSME - Competitiveness of Enterprises and SME	Enterprise, internal market, competition	DG for Internal Market, Industry, Entrepreneurship and SMEs EASME	outside Europe. Among the activities funded by COSME there are also various IPR helpdesk (Intellectual Property Rights) for SMEs. **Support to entrepreneurs** COSME supports entrepreneurs by improving the business training, mentoring, guidance and other support services. These initiatives are aimed in particular at categories of people who may find it difficult to express their full potential, such as young entrepreneurs, women and seniors. The program also aims to help companies to gain access to the opportunities offered by digital technologies. **Best conditions for business** COSME aims to reduce administrative and regulatory burdens on SMEs by creating a favourable business environment. It also helps companies to be competitive, encouraging them to adopt new business models and innovative practices. http://ec.europa.eu/growth/smes/cosme/index_it.htm

Programme	Sector	Managed by	Objectives
Consumer Program	Consumer protection	CHAFEA Consumer, Health, Agriculture and Food Executive Agency	The Program for Consumers 2014-2020 aims to help citizens to fully enjoy their rights as consumers and to support the growth, innovation and objectives of Europe 2020 and to actively participate in the single market. http://ec.europa.eu/chafea/consumers/index.html

ACKNOWLEDGMENTS

A book is never the result of the work of an individual. The one you have in your hands is not an exception. There are many people who over the years have inspired me, trained, supported and believed in me, to my ideas. To all of you thanks. But for some of them I feel the need for special mention: Alessandro Falco, 15 years ago I was just a promising young man with many dreams, you gave me confidence and we still are on business together, we built beautiful things, we'll continue to do so.

My team at work. They are men and women, professionals in European project design and management at the highest level in Europe. Without them not only this book but a lot of what I did, and we did as an Organization, would not be possible.

Among them, a special thanks to Antonella Tozzi, you're already a star in the European projects' firmament, we will continue to do great things together.

I owe a very special mention to Cristine Dover, Faculty of Computing, Engineering and Sciences, Staffordshire University, Science Centre, for the final proof reading of the English version.

Thank you all for your contributions, input, revisions and patience during the creation of this book.

Thanks also to Wolfram Adelmann, Vita Adomaviciute, Tomaz Amon, Rossano Arenare, Carmen Arias, Stefano Arciprete, Linas Atostogoskaime, Simone Baldassarri, Tina Baloh, Maria Gracia Benitez, Olena Bilozerova, Michaela Bitsakis, Federica Bitti, Romain Bocognani, Laura Borlone, Sergio Bornelli, Mariusz Brabal, Raffaele Buompane, Iole Candido, Stefano Carboni, Barbara Casillo, Franja Centrih, Danila Conte, Kathryn Cormican, Giorgio Corradini, Giorgio Costantini, Xenia e Aris Chronopoulos, Cinzia De Marzo, Giorgio De Bin, Gergana Deenichina, Ivana Devic, Milen Dobrev, Kostas Drakas, Lennard Drogendiik, Enver Duz, Vytaute Ezerskiene, John Fairburn, Giancarlo e Marilena Falco, Valeria Fantozzi, Sebastiano Fumero, Tiago Gaio, Andrea Gentili, Nina Georgieva, Mario Giambone, Mustafa Ginesar, Sophie Hanssen, Dogan Incesulu, Mattheos Kakaris, Vaiva Kelmelyte, Kathy Kikis-Papadakis, Maria Kowalewska, Pavol Krempasky, Rosario Improta, Dogan Incesulu, Deirdre Lillis, Antonio Loredan, Ciro Maddaloni, Bruno Marasà, Ernesto Marcheggiani, Elisa Maviglia, Ifigenia Metaxa, Pietro Michelacci, Sebastiano Molaro, Giuseppe Pace, Sara Pagliai, Costanza Patti, Darina Pavelekova, Roxana Pintilescu, Luca Pirozzi, Gianni Pittella, Gianluigi Rossi, Domenico Rossetti di Valdalbero, Robert Sanders, Maren Satke, Przemyslaw Sekalski, Elisabetta Sessa, Nikos Skarmeas, Anna Sobczak, Christian Stracke, Mario Spatafora, Irina Tikhonova, Gianfranco Trerotola, Francesca Tudini, Manon Van Leeuwen, Philippe Vanrie, Eri Vazquez, Valentina Violi, Dilek Volkan, Boguslaw Wozniak, Elena Zarino, Ana Zubcic.

Gianluca Coppola

CPSIA information can be obtained
at www.ICGtesting.com
Printed in the USA
LVHW041655240319
611647LV00017B/985/P

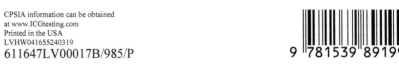

9 781539 891994